CHICAGO

AMERICA'S RAILROAD CAPITAL

THE ILLUSTRATED HISTORY
1836 to Today

Voyageur
Press

Dedication

To all photographers of Chicago's railroads, past and present.

First published in 2014 by Voyageur Press, an imprint of Quarto Publishing Group USA Inc.,
400 First Avenue North, Suite 400, Minneapolis, MN 55401 USA

Voyageur Press titles are also available at discounts in bulk quantity for industrial or sales-promotional use. For details write to Special Sales Manager at Quarto Publishing Group USA Inc., 400 First Avenue North, Suite 400, Minneapolis, MN 55401 USA.

To find out more about our books, visit us online at www.voyageurpress.com.

ISBN-13: 978-0-7603-4603-7

Library of Congress Cataloging-in-Publication Data

Solomon, Brian, 1966- author.
  Chicago : America's railroad capital : the illustrated history, 1836 to today / by Brian Solomon, Michael W. Blaszak, John Gruber, Chris Guss.
       pages cm
"A history of the development of Chicago as a railroad hub, from its earliest days to the present, illustrated with color and black and white photographs, maps, and railroad memorabilia"-Provided by publisher.
  Includes bibliographical references and index.
  ISBN 978-0-7603-4603-7 (hc : alk. paper)
  1. Railroads--Illinois--Chicago--History. 2. Chicago (Ill.)--History. I. Blaszak, Michael W., author.
II. Gruber, John E., 1936- author. III. Guss, Chris, author. IV. Title.
  TF25.C459S65 2014
  385.09773'11--dc23
                        2014012769

Acquisitions Editor: Dennis Pernu
Project Manager: Elizabeth Noll
Art Director: Cindy Samargia Laun
Cover Design: Kent Jensen
Interior Design and Layout: Kim Winscher

On the front cover: Composite view of Chicago then and now. *Black & white photo by Richard Jay Solomon, color skyline by Chris Guss*
On the back cover: Jack Delano's 1940s view of Illinois Central's South Water Street terminal. *Library of Congress*
On the frontis: Metra's 16th Street Tower on the Rock District, Jan 2009. *Chris Guss*
On the title page: Canadian National Train M394 departs downtown on the former Illinois Central. *Ryan Schoenfeldt*

Printed in China

10 9 8 7 6 5 4 3 2 1

CONTENTS

ACKNOWLEDGMENTS

A book on this intricate and detailed subject could not have been produced without help from many people. Over the years countless railroaders, industry professionals, railway historians, librarians, technology enthusiasts, and photographers have aided and guided the authors in their quest for information and a better understanding of Chicago and its trains, locomotives, railway transit, history, and art.

Thanks to: Mike Abalos, Howard Ande, Marshall W. Beecher, William M. Beecher Jr., Paul Behrens, Kurt Bell, Dan Bigda, Jim Boyd, Robert A. Buck, Chris Burger, Joe Burgess, Brian Burns, Paul Carver, David Clinton, Mike Danneman, Tom Danneman, Tim Doherty, John Eagan, Bon French, Sean Graham-White, Dick Gruber, J. Michael Gruber, Don Gulbrandsen, Paul Hammond, John P. Hankey, Mark Hemphill, T. S. Hoover, Thomas M. Hoover, Brian L. Jennison, Clark Johnson Jr., Tom Kline, George W. Kowanski, Blair Kooistra, Bob Krambles, Don Marson, Fred Matthews, Joe McMillan, Arthur Miller, Hal Miller, Bill Molony, Doug Moore, Dan Munson, Mel Patrick, John E. Pickett, Sean Robitaille, Jon Roma, Pete Ruesch, Dean Sauvola, Mike Schafer, J. D. Schmid, Jim Shaughnessy, Gordon Smith, Richard J. Solomon, Sean Solomon, Charles Stats, Vic Stone, Charles Streetman, Carl Swanson, Tom Tancula, Matthew Van Hattem, Otto M. Vondrak, Philip A. Weibler, Craig Willett, Jay Williams, Pat Yough, and Walter Zullig.

Needless to say, any errors are the responsibility of the authors, and not these fine people.

INTRODUCTION

"Although Chicago is the greatest railroad center in the world, there has never been a comprehensive study made by a duly qualified and authorized technical commission of its railroad passenger and freight terminal problem in its entirety." These were the opening words in B. J. Arnold's intensive 250-page study of Chicago's terminals, dated August 18, 1913. Despite the scale of the topic, the author charged forward, offering a detailed examination of Chicago's railways and terminals. Another author faced with the intimidating scale and complexity of Chicago's railroad network, Arthur Curran, writing in the Railway & Locomotive Historical Society's *R&LHS Bulletin* (Issue 40, May 1936), excused his learned paper's omissions with this caveat: "The vast trackage in and near Chicago, including yards and approaches to stations, would require volumes for adequate description." Further, he wrote with humility, "This is a big subject, and the present article is intended more to attract those interested than to make any pretensions of comprehensiveness."

Chicago is more complex in terms of its history, infrastructure, and operations than any other railroad city. Despite innumerable changes in the railroad industry, it remains America's railroad capital. On any given day, about 1,300 trains carrying freight and passengers pulse across its urban landscape. As authors of this book, we have accepted the challenge of distilling this immense topic into one concise, illustrated volume. The four of us have taken four independent approaches intended to give the reader a thoroughly detailed, if not all-inclusive, understanding of the railroad city that works. Together we have pored over hundreds of sources; met with dozens of railway experts, railroaders, and Chicagoans; and reviewed thousands of images. What you have here is a starting point for understanding how Chicago's railroads came to be and how they operate today.

We have focused on the main lines, while giving a cursory treatment to the famous Insull interurbans and touching upon Chicago's extensive rapid transit and streetcar system. These latter subjects are worthy topics for books of their own, many of which have been written. Readers will forgive us for not delving into the intriguing tale of Chicago's long-abandoned underground narrow gauge freight subway.

We hope that this book will explain Chicago's railroads in ways never before achieved, and that the text and photos will further your understanding of America's greatest railroad city. Enjoy!

CHAPTER 1

Chicago Railway History

By Michael W. Blaszak

Chicago. The word is a French interpretation of the Native American term for the odorous plants that lined the marshy shores of the city's namesake river. It's an appropriate name, since water is the primary reason the city developed where it did.

When French explorers Jacques Marquette and Louis Jolliet paddled their canoes down the Mississippi River from Wisconsin in 1673, the Illini tribes showed them a shortcut back to their base in Quebec. This route to Lake Michigan, via the Illinois and Des Plaines Rivers and a brief portage to the South Branch of the Chicago River, became a key link between the French colonies in Canada and Louisiana and opened the land west of the lake to the voyageurs' fur trade.

Ninety years later, the land passed from the French to the British, and then to the fledgling United States of America at the end of the American Revolution in 1783, becoming part of the Northwest Territory in 1787. The indigenous people of the Chicago area, primarily of the Potawatomi tribe, ceded a six-square-mile parcel of land at the mouth of the Chicago River to the United States in 1795. In 1803 the federal government built Fort Dearborn.

Opposite Page: Nickel Plate Road's *New Yorker* departs LaSalle Street Station. (See page 39.) *Richard Jay Solomon*

The last of the four Ice Age ice sheets, known as the Laurentide, began forming about one hundred thousand years ago. By eighteen thousand years ago the ice sheet, over two miles thick, covered almost all of modern-day Canada and reached south to the current Chicago area. As the climate warmed, the ice sheet retreated. Over time, the melting ice left behind today's Great Lakes. Looking northeast toward Lake Michigan, Norfolk Southern Railway's 55th Street Yards are at the center right; the old Union Stock Yards once extended to the area at far left. Prior to 1976, the Erie/Erie Lackawanna 47th Street Yard was located in this area. *Sean Graham-White*

A City, a Canal, and a Rail Line: Galena & Chicago Union Railroad

Jean Baptiste Point du Sable, generally recognized as Chicago's first permanent resident, migrated to the swampy land along the Chicago River in the 1780s to trade with the Native Americans. Migration intensified after the Erie Canal linked the Great Lakes with the populated Atlantic Seaboard in 1825. Another canal from the Chicago River to the Illinois River would extend waterborne commerce across the Chicago portage to the Mississippi River basin. The state of Illinois, admitted to the Union in 1818, began organizing a canal in 1829 with Chicago at its eastern terminus. Here a town was located near the confluence

of the river's North and South Branches in 1830. By 1837, a year after work on the Illinois & Michigan (I&M) Canal had commenced, the population of the new city of Chicago had grown from 50 to 4,170. The ninety-six-mile I&M Canal opened on April 23, 1848.

William Butler Ogden was among Chicago's new citizens, having moved there from New York. Legend has it that, while standing in ankle-deep mud and grumpily assessing the Chicago property his brother-in-law had bought, he complained, "You have been guilty of the grossest folly." Yet Ogden recognized potential in Chicago's strategic location and bought land himself. Upon the city's incorporation in 1837, he was elected its first mayor. He would become a driving influence behind many Chicago railroads over the following decades.

Ogden first became involved in the construction of a railroad west from Chicago, where topography made a canal impractical. It was the Galena & Chicago Union Railroad (G&CU), which later became part of the Chicago & North Western Railway (C&NW). The G&CU was organized in 1836 to connect Chicago with the lead mining town of Galena in Illinois' northwest corner, but financial difficulties stalled it until Ogden revived it 1847. His Chicago Group sold stock door-to-door to people who might benefit directly from the new line. Construction began in June 1848 on Chicago's western edge at Kinzie and Halsted Streets. The line's first engine was a diminutive secondhand 4-2-0 Baldwin wood-burner christened the Pioneer that arrived by boat on October 10, 1848. G&CU's first revenue trains carried wheat and dressed hogs to Chicago in December 1848. Two years later the Aurora Branch Railroad, starting from its namesake city on the Fox River, connected to the G&CU at "the Junction" (today's West Chicago), while G&CU's main line extended to Elgin in 1850 and Rockford two years later.

Chicago & North Western Railway antecedent Galena & Chicago Union Railroad began construction in June 1848 and reached Elgin, Illinois, in 1850. This evolved into an important commuter line, as well as a key transcontinental link when C&NW extended to Omaha, Nebraska, and Council Bluffs, Iowa, to meet Union Pacific Railroad (UP). Unique to C&NW were home-modified Crandall Cabs rebuilt from old UP B-units for suburban service. *Bon French*

The Longest Railroad: Illinois Central

Illinois enjoys an abundance of navigable waterways. The Mississippi forms its western boundary, the Ohio and Wabash Rivers define its southeastern flank, and the Illinois River and its tributaries cut across the state diagonally. But river travel is slow and circuitous, so in 1837 the state legislature passed the Illinois Internal Improvements Act to fund construction of 1,300 miles of state-owned railroads.

Chief among these proposed lines was the Illinois Central Railroad (IC), to run from Cairo at the state's southern tip to Galena in the northwest. Four east-west lines were projected to add ribs to this spine. One of these,

the Northern Cross Railroad, became the first railroad to lay track in the state in 1838, from the Illinois River port of Meredosia toward the new capital in Springfield. Opened in 1842, the fifty-five-mile line eventually became part of the Wabash Railroad (WAB).

Illinois abandoned its Central Railroad project before laying a single rail, and private enterprise had all but given up on it by 1845. Then Stephen A. Douglas took charge. He was a lawyer, judge, and politician who by 1847 had risen to the U.S. Senate. Douglas was a man who got things done. In 1848, he moved to Chicago and began buying real estate on the South Side, while using his political position to resuscitate the Central Railroad through a federal land grant. He sponsored

Illinois Central's *Louisiane* was a secondary long-distance train on the Chicago–New Orleans route. It carried coaches from New Orleans, Louisiana, and sleepers from Memphis, Tennessee. Here the *Louisiane,* train No. 4, is seen at 18th Street on its approach to Central Station on the morning of September 7, 1958. *Walter E. Zullig*

Illinois Central's Weldon Coach Yard as viewed on an afternoon in September 1971. *George W. Kowanski*

legislation to extend the main line from Galena to Dunleith (today's East Dubuque) on the Mississippi while adding a branch through his Chicago landholdings. President Millard Fillmore signed Douglas' land grant bill on September 20, 1850, and the Illinois legislature granted IC a state charter to build its system on February 10, 1851.

IC commenced construction southward from 22nd Street in Chicago in 1852, but controversy over its route north of 22nd Street slowed progress. The railroad wanted to build along the South Branch of the Chicago River on Chicago's West Side, but politicians had another idea. The comfortable houses of the city's elite lined Michigan Avenue, and the city had been forced to spend large sums to keep the lake from

washing the street away. Why not transfer this headache to the new railroad in return for the right to lay track on a trestle along the lakeshore? The railroad reluctantly agreed, and on December 3, 1853, IC's first over-water train reached its terminal on the grounds of old Fort Dearborn.

IC's charter lines were completed by 1856, and the 705-mile system was briefly the nation's longest railroad under unified management. When IC's Great Central Station, a brick six-track passenger terminal and headquarters office, opened on South Water Street on June 21 of that year, it was Chicago's largest building. A month later, IC introduced local trains to serve a new residential development at Hyde Park— Chicago's first commuter service.

First Railroad to the Mississippi: the Rock Island

In Rock Island, Illinois, a town on the Mississippi River, a railroad was born when local businessmen organized the Rock Island & La Salle Railroad in 1847. They aimed to build due east across the prairie and meet the I&M Canal. When the railroad's finances stalled, management sought help from Henry Farnam, an experienced railroad contractor, who recommended extending the railroad to Chicago to link with projected lines from the East. The railroad's charter was amended to rename the company the Chicago & Rock Island Railroad, nicknamed the Rock Island. Construction commenced in October 1851, using fifty-seven-pound iron rail rolled in England. The first forty miles, from 22nd Street in Chicago to Joliet, Illinois (on the Des Plaines River), were completed within a year. On October 10, 1852,

a brand-new Rogers-built 4-4-0, appropriately named Rocket, led Rock Island's first official passenger train to Joliet in two hours. Then it reversed direction back to Chicago, because Joliet lacked turning facilities.

By February 22, 1854, the Rock Island had reached its namesake town, making it the first railroad to link Chicago with the Mississippi River. Meanwhile, the first bridge across the Mississippi was under construction to carry the Rock into Iowa. When a steamboat collided with the bridge in 1856, Rock Island hired a prominent lawyer named Abraham Lincoln to defend it against the steamboat owner's claim for damages. Lincoln's skill in winning dismissal of the lawsuit propelled him into a campaign against Stephen A. Douglas for the Senate. Lincoln lost, but the fame he earned while debating Douglas made him a viable—and ultimately successful—presidential candidate in 1860.

Rock Island used one of General Motors Electro-Motive Division's futuristic looking LWT-12 diesels to power its *Talgo* train, seen here approaching Chicago's Englewood Union Station in 1961. The LWT-12 also powered GM's own *Aerotrain*, another train the Rock Island operated. *Richard Jay Solomon*

In June 1961, a New York Central E-unit glides to a stop at Englewood. This station was discontinued as a long-distance stop with the coming of Amtrak, and the area deteriorated rapidly. By the 1980s it was suffering from urban blight. Englewood is unrecognizable to longtime railroad observers today, with the grade separation of Metra's Rock Island Line and Norfolk Southern in progress during 2013–2014. *Richard Jay Solomon*

First Rail Connections to the East

Chicago's earliest railways aimed to link developing Illinois farmlands with the city and with eastern markets via the Great Lakes. But all-rail transport began to compete with rail-and-water transport as new railroads advanced westward from the East Coast toward Lake Michigan, a natural barrier that forced them toward Chicago. The Buffalo & Mississippi Railroad began construction across Indiana in 1837, but a financial panic that year halted work. A decade passed before new investors, led by William B. Ogden, took control—and they were still unable to build the line.

Michigan's effort to build a statewide canal and railroad network included a southern rail route that extended from Monroe on Lake Erie across the Lower Peninsula to New Buffalo on Lake Michigan. By 1846, the state sold this line to the Michigan Southern Railroad, a company controlled by Edwin C. Litchfield

and his brother Elisha. They leased the Erie & Kalamazoo Railroad in 1849 to reach Toledo, Ohio, and gained control of the moribund Buffalo & Mississippi project, which had been renamed the Northern Indiana Railroad. The Litchfields hired Henry Farnam to build their railroads, and Farnam's connections with the Rock Island established a long-term alliance between these carriers, which survived long after the Litchfields' lines had been melded into larger systems.

In 1851, Northern Indiana Railroad built around the south end of Lake Michigan, and in January 1852 it met Rock Island's line under construction at Junction Grove (now Englewood). North from Englewood the railroads shared tracks to Chicago. The first Michigan Southern locomotive reached Chicago on February 20, 1852, with the first through Toledo–Chicago passenger trains arriving on May 22. By January 1853, a direct rail link between Cleveland and Toledo had been

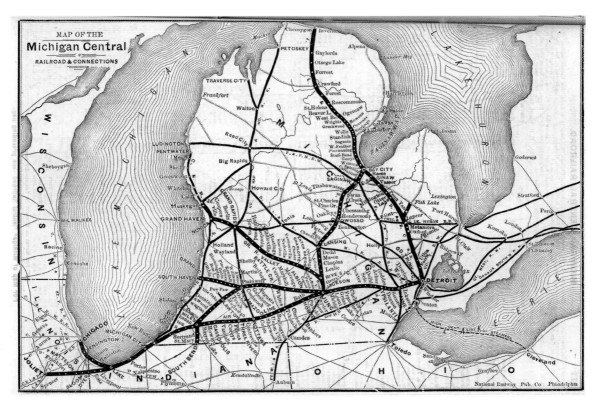

Above: Michigan Central's map from 1875. In its formative years Michigan Central and the Lake Shore & Michigan Southern were bitter rivals that competed for the honor of Chicago's first railroad connection to the East. They became corporate siblings under Vanderbilt control within a generation of their inception. Notice the Michigan Central had lines to both Chicago and Joliet. *Buck collection;* **Below:** During the early years of the twentieth century, the city of Chicago and its railroads undertook a cooperative effort to elevate many main lines in densely populated areas. Here the grade separation of the joint Fort Wayne (PRR)/Lake Shore & Michigan Southern (NYC) over the Illinois Central and 76th Street is under construction. The Nickel Plate (then owned by NYC) will snake under the PRR/NYC elevation to the left of the IC and join the Lake Shore to reach LaSalle Street Station. *John Gruber collection*

completed, which opened a continuous rail route from Boston and New York to Chicago.

Michigan's state-financed rail system also included a central route that had been sold to the Michigan Central Railroad (MC). Built in competition with the Litchfields' lines, MC stalled when it reached Michigan City, Indiana, in October 1850 because Northern Indiana Railroad lobbyists delayed legislation authorizing construction westward. Ultimately, MC reached an alliance with Illinois Central Railroad to enter Chicago, causing IC to build south of Chicago in early 1852 to meet MC. When Northern Indiana tried to stymie MC's plan by rejecting IC's request to cross its line, IC dispatched employees under cover of darkness to install a diamond at what later became known as Grand Crossing, completing the through MC–IC route between Detroit and Chicago on May 21, 1852.

With these new eastern rail connections, Chicago boomed. In April 1855, an amazing twenty-two-car Northern Indiana train discharged more than one thousand passengers into the city. Chicago's population tripled between 1850 and 1860.

Despite their early rivalry, both Michigan-based eastern connections were absorbed into the New York Central System (NYC). Northern Indiana merged with Michigan Southern and in 1869 was folded into the Lake Shore & Michigan Southern Railway (LSMS). That same year, New York financier Jay Gould vied with Cornelius Vanderbilt for control of the LSMS, but Vanderbilt prevailed. Under his son, William H. Vanderbilt, NYC took control of MC in 1878.

The Strange Saga of the St. Charles Air Line

Railroads don't like competition. But Chicago's pioneer carriers faced lots of it as promoters floated myriad schemes to build competing lines. The St. Charles Branch Railroad was chartered in 1849 and was renamed the Chicago, St. Charles & Mississippi Air Line

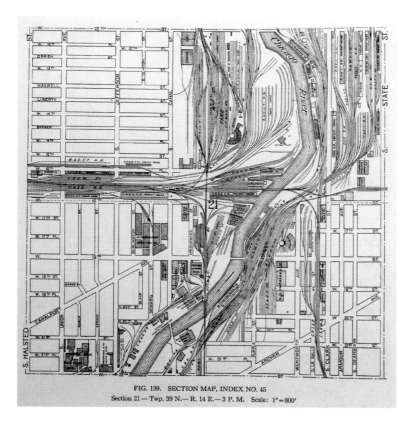

FIG. 139. SECTION MAP, INDEX NO. 45
Section 21 — Twp. 39 N.— R. 14 E.— 3 P. M. Scale: 1″=800′

This map (from the 1915 electrification study) shows the west end of the St. Charles Air Line and the historic terminal facilities along the South Branch of the Chicago River before the river was straightened in 1928–1929. Note the freight houses, used to handle less-than-carload traffic, and the grain elevators for transferring agricultural shipments from rail to water, all of which are long gone. The Schoenhofen Brewery, though, survives today after impersonating an orphanage in the 1980 movie *The Blues Brothers*. *Mike Blaszak collection*

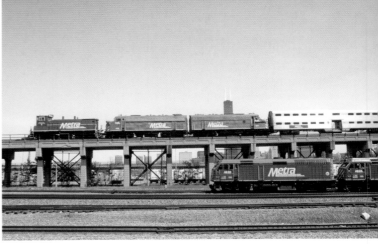

Left: A motley assortment of locomotives lead an Illinois Central freight train towards 16th Street Tower on March 20, 1990, where it will enter the St. Charles Air Line. The middle of the train is passing through 21st Street (Fort Wayne Junction) interlocking, with the tower just above the third locomotive in the distance. Just north of 21st Street is the bridge across the South Branch of the Chicago River. *Mike Abalos;* **Right:** On May 20, 1999, a Metra work extra on the St. Charles Air Line features one of its rarely photographed SW 1500 switchers and its lone pair of former Chicago & North Western F7s. On the lower level, a pair of F40PHM-2s (a model unique to Metra) leads an Aurora-bound train. *Mike Abalos*

Railroad (commonly called the St. Charles Air Line) in 1853. (*Air line* was a popular term indicating a straight and direct railroad.) The St. Charles Air Line was projected to build from the South Branch of the Chicago River (around 15th Street) west-northwest via St. Charles (on the Fox River) across Illinois to Savanna on the Mississippi River, where it would connect with another projected line in Iowa.

However, the Galena & Chicago Union, plotting its own line to the Mississippi, was hostile to the St. Charles Air Line project. In an age without antitrust laws and federal regulation, the G&CU simply bought the Air Line on April 10, 1854. Under G&CU ownership, the Air Line was built just nine miles from the South Branch west to a junction with the G&CU's main line at Harlem (today's Oak Park) by 1855, but no farther west. By 1864, a north-south cutoff along Rockwell Street (today Union Pacific's Rockwell Subdivision) superseded the Harlem link, making that line one of Chicago's first abandoned railroads.

But the Air Line name lives on for a quite different reason. In their original configurations, Chicago's initial railroads—G&CU and its tenant Aurora Branch (renamed Chicago & Aurora in 1852), the Rock Island–Northern Indiana joint line, and the Illinois Central–Michigan Central joint line—didn't connect with each other despite having been built to the common 4'8½" standard gauge. Yet a connection would be mutually advantageous.

Boston capitalists led by John Murray Forbes had both backed the Michigan Central and invested in the Aurora Branch, which gave them the incentive to construct a link between Illinois Central (used by MC) and G&CU (Chicago & Aurora's link to Chicago) using the St. Charles Air Line and a new extension eastward over the South Branch of the Chicago River to the IC tracks at the lakefront. Opened in 1856, the connection became known as the St. Charles Air Line, even though the eastward extension never was owned by the original company of that name.

In 1855, Chicago & Aurora was renamed Chicago, Burlington & Quincy (CB&Q), and CB&Q, G&CU, IC, and MC shared equal ownership of the new Air Line link. Despite a century and a half of changes in Chicago railroading, these lines' respective successors—Burlington Northern Santa Fe (BNSF), Union Pacific, and Canadian National (CN, which acquired the MC share)—continue to own the strategic St. Charles Air Line connection. IC was (and still is, under the CN name) responsible for maintaining and dispatching the Air Line. When the Air Line opened, CB&Q (and briefly, G&CU) used it to send passenger trains to IC's Great Central Station.

Rails to Wisconsin: Origins of the Chicago & North Western

In 1848, Wisconsin became a U.S. state, and soon after, it granted railroad charters to encourage interior settlement. The Madison & Beloit Railroad (soon renamed Rock River Valley Union Railroad or RRVU) envisioned a route from the Illinois state line northward to Lake Winnebago. To reach Chicago, it anticipated a connection with Galena & Chicago Union at Crystal Lake, Illinois (a few miles south of the Wisconsin border). But G&CU's route avoided Crystal Lake, and RRVU incorporated its own Chicago connection called the Illinois & Wisconsin Railroad (I&W). Bizarrely, this system was originally envisioned as a six-foot gauge line because chief engineer E. C. Johnson had worked at the New York & Erie (NY&E), America's premier broad gauge railroad. Historians debate whether any broad gauge track was actually laid, but if it was, that track was quickly converted to standard gauge.

Illinois & Wisconsin defaulted in early 1853, and Ogden (who had left the G&CU in 1851) joined a group that assumed control of the line. In April 1855, Ogden merged RRVU and I&W to form the Chicago, St. Paul & Fond du Lac Railroad, which was reorganized as Chicago & North-Western Railroad (the company later dropped the hyphen) after the 1857 financial panic. The 176-mile Chicago–Fond du Lac line opened in 1859.

Above: Color photos taken in the early 1960s through telephoto lenses are rare. Richard J. Solomon made this image of an outbound Chicago & North Western suburban train on Kodachrome using a Kodak Retina 3C fitted with a Schneider Xenon 90mm lens. Chicago's Merchandise Mart, occupying the former site of C&NW's Wells Street Station, looms in the distance. *Richard Jay Solomon;* **Below:** A Chicago & North Western GP7 leads an outbound commuter train. C&NW's North Western Station was an early application of all-electric signaling. Instead of the mechanical signaling commonly employed when the station opened in 1911, state-of-the-art electrically operated semaphores governed train movements. *Richard Jay Solomon;* **Button:** *O. P. Jones collection*

In 1851 another line called the Green Bay, Milwaukee & Chicago Railroad was chartered to build a north-south railroad from Milwaukee, Wisconsin, to the Illinois state line, while another company, named the Illinois Parallel Railroad, was chartered in Illinois to extend the Wisconsin line to Chicago, paralleling the Lake Michigan shore. Ease of construction enabled the two companies to complete their eighty-five-mile Chicago–Milwaukee route in the spring of 1855, introducing a through Chicago–Milwaukee passenger service with two daily trains in each direction. Relations between the unrelated halves of this route weren't always harmonious. For a period around 1860, they discontinued this service and forced through patrons to walk across the state line from one train to the other. This was bad for business, though, and the two firms soon overcame their differences and merged under the Chicago & Milwaukee Railway name in 1863. Under Ogden's management, C&NW merged with G&CU in 1864, and two years later the new C&NW absorbed the Chicago & Milwaukee as well, giving it a third main line into Chicago.

The Fort Wayne Route: Pennsylvania Railroad Reaches Chicago

Pennsylvania publicly financed a transportation system called the Main Line of Public Works, a 394-mile network of canals and railroads aimed at developing that state's interior. When completed in 1834, the Main Line cut travel time from Philadelphia to Pittsburgh (on the Ohio River) over the Allegheny Mountains to four days. Yet the Main Line proved slow and costly, and in 1846 the Pennsylvania Railroad (PRR) was incorporated to replace it. By 1854 PRR's main line was open over the Allegheny Summit by way of Horseshoe Curve, but the company's ambitions soon included a Chicago extension.

PRR used its influence to combine three budding short lines as the Pittsburgh, Fort Wayne & Chicago Railway on August 1, 1856. The Fort Wayne line reached Chicago on January 1, 1859. Overcoming initial financial woes, which resulted in the appointment of Ogden as the company's receiver, the Fort Wayne had to build a second

A Pennsylvania Railroad long-distance train reverses into Chicago Union Station for loading on a warm June 1961 afternoon. The lack of heavy head-end traffic is an indication that this may be PRR's premier *Broadway Limited,* which departed Chicago at 5:00 p.m. *Richard Jay Solomon*

main track to handle Civil War business. After the war ended, Gould, who controlled the competing New York & Erie, bought into the Fort Wayne, but PRR regained control and secured it with a 999-year lease.

In Illinois, the Fort Wayne ran parallel to New York Central System's Lake Shore & Michigan Southern main line between the Indiana–Illinois state line and Englewood, then turned north, entering Chicago along the west bank of the South Branch of the Chicago River. The Fort Wayne bought two blocks along the riverbank between Madison and Adams Streets for its terminal. This property would be included in the footprint of today's Chicago Union Station.

A Link to St. Louis: Chicago & Alton

St. Louis, Missouri, was founded by French settlers in 1764 and grew rapidly with the development of steamboat transportation. It remained substantially more populous than Chicago through the 1850s. In February 1850, the Alton & Sangamon Railroad was chartered to construct a seventy-two-mile line from Alton, Illinois (a Mississippi port upriver from St. Louis) to the Illinois state capital at Springfield. Before the new road's first train reached Springfield on September 9, 1852,

the state had approved a proposed extension to Bloomington and Chicago.

The Litchfield brothers joined the enterprise, supplying finances, material, and equipment to build the line northward. On July 31, 1854, its first train arrived at Joliet after a twelve-hour journey from Alton. The railroad was later renamed the St. Louis, Alton & Chicago and then the Chicago & Alton (C&A), but it was commonly known as simply the Alton.

Initially, Rock Island handled Alton's passenger trains between Joliet and Chicago, while freight was transferred to boats on the Illinois & Michigan Canal. However, soon connecting railroads were built to supersede the inefficient canal connection. In 1855, the Joliet & Northern Indiana constructed a forty-five-mile line eastward to Lake Station, Indiana, to connect with its parent company, Michigan Central, while the city of Lockport, Illinois (located a few miles north of Joliet), organized the Joliet & Chicago Railroad (J&C) to supplement the I&M Canal. The Alton leased this latter route, which reached Chicago in 1858. J&C's inauspicious ceremonial first train left Joliet on March 18, but derailed twice in Bridgeport, Chicago, before finally reaching its destination that evening with two brass bands on board. To secure Chicago terminal facilities, Alton teamed with the Fort Wayne; the J&C bought a half interest in the Fort Wayne's South Branch Chicago River bridge and its line to Van Buren

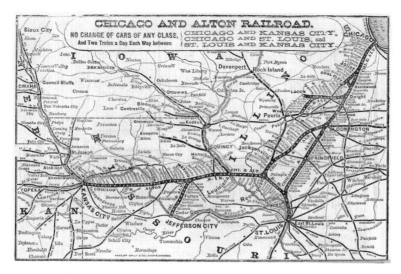

A map of the Chicago & Alton system from 1881. The Alton & Sangamon Railroad was chartered in 1850. Later renamed St. Louis, Alton, & Chicago and again renamed Chicago & Alton, it was commonly known as simply the Alton. Today the St. Louis–Joliet portion is operated by Union Pacific, and the portion from Joliet to Chicago by Canadian National. This is Amtrak's route to St. Louis. *Buck collection*

Street. Initially, Alton passenger trains used the St. Charles Air Line to reach Illinois Central's Great Central Station, but moved west when the Fort Wayne built its second station on the west side of the river in 1863 (the first station, built in 1861, burned down the following year). Alton and its successors remained a tenant of the current Union Station site until the eve of Amtrak more than a century later.

Burlington Builds a Direct Route

The Chicago, Burlington & Quincy soon became dissatisfied with its access to Chicago over the Galena & Chicago Union. Even though by 1857 G&CU had double-tracked its thirty-mile route to CB&Q's connection, heavy traffic resulted in continued congestion, and G&CU controlled operations to its advantage. In 1862, following years of disputes, CB&Q stockholders approved building a direct route from Aurora,

Above: A view from a Chicago Transit Authority (CTA) Orange Line train bound for Midway International Airport finds a southward (eastbound) stack train led by Chicago & North Western SD60s crossing the Illinois Central (former Alton route) diamonds at Brighton Park on January 1, 1995. *Brian Solomon;* **Below:** Gulf, Mobile & Ohio Railroad (GM&O) reached Chicago after World War II, when it acquired the Alton route from Baltimore & Ohio Railroad (B&O). Alton's tenancy at Union Station stemmed from its early terminal arrangements with the Fort Wayne route in the 1860s. GM&O's *Abraham Lincoln* approaches Union Station on April 24, 1971, on the eve of Amtrak, which took over this train on May 1 that year. On the right are Burlington Northern's 14th Street Coach Yards, and beyond is the 21st Street Bridge over the South Branch of the Chicago River. *John Gruber*

An A-B-A F3/FT set leads a Burlington freight on its busy three-track raceway west of Lisle, Illinois. Burlington's line from Aurora to Chicago was (and is) one of the Chicago area's most heavily used routes. Burlington's early relationship with Electro-Motive matured as the builder flourished. Electro-Motive's primary locomotive plant at McCook was built near Burlington's main line in 1935–1936; and from the Zephyrs to SD45s, Burlington was a buyer of Electro-Motive products. *George Spier*

Illinois, east to the St. Charles Air Line bridge in Chicago. Construction commenced in October 1862 and required an expensive fill across the marshy headwaters of Flagg Creek (between today's Western Springs and Hinsdale). The line opened on May 20, 1864, with its easterly ten miles double-tracked the following year.

CB&Q's Chicago extension included seventy-five acres along the South Branch of the Chicago River, where the railroad built freight houses, grain elevators, yards, and a roundhouse. At that time, lake boats carried large volumes of lumber into, and grain out of, Chicago. To expedite transfers, CB&Q built tracks directly to the river slips via an arrangement with the South Branch Dock Company. The Chicago area was rapidly becoming a meat-processing center, and CB&Q handled large volumes of cattle and hogs. However, a proposed forty-acre livestock terminal near Aurora was shelved in favor of a more ambitious stockyard scheme.

Union Stock Yards

By 1864 seven stockyards were in operation along rail lines on Chicago's South Side. (Madison Avenue divides the North and South Sides.) These stockyards were scattered from a location on the Fort Wayne (south of 12th Street where the Amtrak coach yard is today) to a stretch of the lakefront known as Cleaverville, south all the way to Brighton Park on the Alton. Civil War disruptions of north-south trade benefited Chicago's meatpackers; the city surpassed the one-time "Porkopolis"—Cincinnati, Ohio—as the nation's leading slaughterer of hogs, with 970,000 animals processed in 1862–1863. Most of the meatpacking plants congregated outside the city limits along a tributary of the South Branch, which became known as Bubbly Creek from effluences of rotting offal dumped in the water.

The burgeoning meat business employed many Chicago newcomers and enriched its

An eastward Illinois Central local on the former Alton hammers the crossing at Brighton Park on December 18, 1994. Until 2007, this was one of the last complex non-interlocked crossings in North America where all trains were required to stop and manually operated mechanical semaphores were used to signal trains to proceed. *Brian Solomon*

capitalists. But byproducts and waste polluted the river and produced an awful stench, as did piles of excrement dropped by cattle and hogs being driven through the streets from stockyards to abattoirs. The smell and filth made the business extremely unpopular. To appease the public, meatpackers suggested consolidating the stockyards and packing plants at a single location on the city's fringe, and the railroads concurred.

Union Stock Yards & Transit Company was authorized on February 13, 1865; nine railroads subscribed to 92.5 percent of its stock. The company secured 320 marshy acres at Halsted and 39th Street, drained the water, and built wooden stock pens. The new stockyards opened on Christmas Day that year. A connecting railroad was built from a lakefront junction with Illinois Central west through the new stockyards and north from Brighton Park to the North Western's original St. Charles Air Line near 14th Street. The company allowed its railroad owners

to operate over this new line, assigning each railroad an area to unload livestock.

The Union Stock Yards were an immediate success fueled by the rapid expansion of railroads through the Great Plains, which brought in livestock from as far away as Texas to be converted into steaks and hides. Gustavus Swift's perfection of the refrigerator car in 1878, using ice and brine to control temperature, facilitated long-distance shipments of meat from Chicago to destinations across the East and South. Under an 1890 reorganization, the stockyards railroad was renamed Chicago Junction Railway. In 1922 New York Central purchased the Chicago River & Indiana Railroad, which operated thirty-seven miles of industrial lines from the stockyards to Elsdon, which in turn leased the Chicago Junction. Chicago's other railroads retained the right to operate directly into the Stock Yards, which closed in 1971.

The Panhandle: PRR's Link to the South

In 1853, The Cincinnati, Logansport & Chicago Railway built a 26.79-mile line between Richmond and New Castle, Indiana, with visions of connecting Chicago and Cincinnati. By 1861 related companies extended the line west via Logansport to Fort Wayne Junction with the Pittsburgh, Fort Wayne & Chicago near Valparaiso, Indiana. This line was soon reorganized as the Cincinnati & Chicago Air-Line Railroad. It offered mail and express trains over its 280-mile through route between its namesake cities, using the Fort Wayne to access Chicago.

Dissatisfaction with the Fort Wayne led to the organizing of the first of four Chicago & Great Eastern Railway (C&GE) companies in Indiana on June 19, 1863, to provide a direct route to Chicago. In 1865, C&GE consolidated with a dormant Illinois corporation called Galena & Illinois River Railroad to create the second C&GE. Two more corporate iterations of the C&GE brought the Air-Line into the fold, and the combined company built a 64.86-mile link northwest from LaCrosse, Indiana, later that year.

Chicago's intense urbanization made direct entry to downtown prohibitively expensive, so C&GE built a circuitous route, crossing the Illinois Central at Riverdale and the Rock Island at Washington Heights (103rd Street) before heading due north along Western Avenue to C&NW's former Galena & Chicago Union main line (connecting with the Union Stock Yards near 39th Street, or Brighton Park). Reaching the G&CU, C&GE turned east and finally south to a junction with the Fort Wayne in the vicinity of the current Union Station.

In 1868, consolidation of C&GE with other lines formed the Columbus, Chicago &

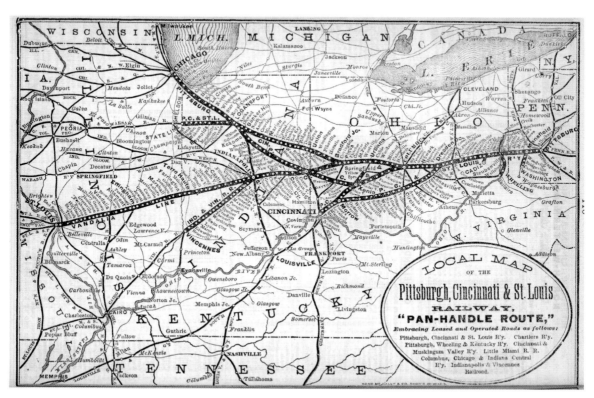

This Panhandle map dates from 1885. The Pittsburgh, Cincinnati & St. Louis Railroad was known as the Panhandle because its Pittsburgh–Columbus line crossed the northern extremity of the newly admitted state of West Virginia. The Panhandle was affiliated with the Pennsylvania Railroad. *Buck collection*

Indiana Central Railway, which was leased to Pittsburgh, Cincinnati & St. Louis Railroad, a PRR affiliate better known as the Panhandle because its Pittsburgh–Columbus main line crossed the northern extremity of the newly admitted state of West Virginia. Between 1885 and 1887, the Panhandle expanded its Chicago connections with PRR by building the Englewood Connecting Railway and South Chicago & Southern Railroad (SC&S). In 1890, the Panhandle was renamed the Pittsburgh, Cincinnati, Chicago & St. Louis Railroad, which eventually was absorbed by PRR.

The Chicago, Danville & Vincennes Railroad (CD&V) began building an independent railroad southward from a connection with the Panhandle at Dolton, Illinois on May 21, 1869. CD&V reached Danville, Illinois, on November 16, 1871, and planned extensions into the southern Indiana coalfields. However, the financial panic of 1873 bankrupted the company. The affiliated Chicago & Southern Railroad was formed to build an independent connection

for the CD&V from Dolton to Chicago via Blue Island. At least one surviving timetable shows this line in operation by 1875, but CD&V's owners lost control of the enterprise. On September 1, 1877, New York investors reorganized the CD&V as the Chicago & Eastern Illinois Railroad (C&EI).

The Chicago Fire

The Great Chicago Fire was—and remains—one of the city's epochal events. It began about 9:00 p.m. on October 8, 1871, at Patrick O'Leary's house at 137 DeKoven Street. The fire consumed building after building in the O'Learys' modest working-class neighborhood—just blocks from the Fort Wayne's main line—though ironically, the O'Learys' own house survived. A fire alarm was pulled at 9:40, but the firemen set off in the wrong direction. Before they could respond, flames had reached the docks along the South Branch of the Chicago River, where coal

In July 1958, this northward Rock Island suburban train pauses for a station stop on the main line at Blue Island. Rock Island augmented its main line to Blue Island with a secondary route for suburban traffic, completed in 1870. During the 1950s, Rock Island's schedule showed more than forty weekday commuter roundtrips between LaSalle Street Station and Blue Island using its Suburban Line, with an additional eighteen roundtrips via its main line. *Richard Jay Solomon*

and lumber awaiting shipment, as well as the wooden ships themselves, accelerated the blaze.

Autumn 1871 had been warm and dry, so the city's mostly wooden buildings—even its sidewalks and streets were made of wood—offered little resistance to the advancing conflagration. Strong southwesterly winds carried the fire across the river to ravenously consume downtown. Chicago's firefighters were completely overmatched; residents were forced to flee into newly created Lincoln Park, or stand knee-deep in the cooling waters of the lake, until the fire (with the help of a rainstorm) burned itself out on October 10. The death toll was estimated at only three hundred, but the city's property was nearly a total loss. From DeKoven Street to Fullerton Avenue, some thirty-four blocks to the north, only a few masonry shells survived.

Chicago's railroads did not escape the destruction. On the morning of October 9, IC general freight agent Joseph Tucker realized that Great Central Station was directly in the path of the blaze. He prevailed on operating management to pull as much equipment as possible southward to safety. The fire destroyed Rock Island's LaSalle Street Station, set IC's lakefront trestle on fire, and reduced Great Central Station to a smoldering ruin. But the Fort Wayne's station survived, the IC and Michigan Central continued operating to 22nd Street, and the Burlington began using a vacant icehouse at 16th and Indiana as its temporary station. Within a few months, IC's trestle was restored and Great Central Station reopened, conveying trains with bricks and lumber to rebuild the city.

Although Chicago rebounded quickly, fear of a recurrence caused many residents to move to the city's perimeter, sparking a suburban boom. The population dispersal increased demand for suburban passenger service, and many railroads took advantage of this new traffic. In 1870, Rock Island had completed its Suburban Line, built west of the original main from Washington Heights to Blue Island, anticipating the suburban exodus. IC's commuter ridership increased 600 percent between 1870 and 1880, expanding the schedule from six weekday trains to thirty-six. IC also extended commuter service to Homewood by 1890 and opened new branches: 69th Street to South Chicago in 1882, and Kensington to Blue Island in 1893.

Enter the St. Paul

The Milwaukee & St. Paul Railroad was the successor to Milwaukee's first rail line, operating three routes across Wisconsin. At first its primary eastern connection was via Lake Michigan boats, but as the 1860s drew to a close, it sought an all-rail alternative. The problem for the St. Paul, as the company was known, was that its only eastward rail connection at Milwaukee was the Chicago & North Western, which was itself rapidly expanding across Wisconsin. C&NW wanted to keep through shipments on its lines as far as it could, rather than maximizing the St. Paul's

Metra's Tower A2 controls the crossing of Metra's Milwaukee Road lines out of Union Station and Union Pacific's Geneva Subdivision out of the Ogilvie Transportation Center (on the site of North Western Station). It is a surviving example of a Union Switch & Signal Model 14 electro-pneumatic interlocking. Originally a Milwaukee Road tower, it was built in 1938 to Pennsylvania Railroad specifications because Milwaukee shared PRR's Panhandle line to reach Union Station. This arrangement stemmed from the 1870s, when the Chicago, Milwaukee & St. Paul Railway bought a half interest in the Panhandle's line to access downtown. *Brian Solomon*

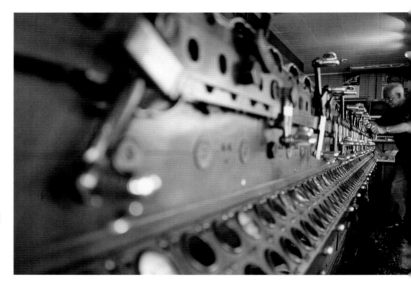

mileage (and revenue) by interchanging at Milwaukee. The solution was obvious: the St. Paul needed to build its own line to Chicago for direct interchange with the eastern and southern railroads.

Plans for this extension commenced before the fire, and construction began southward from Milwaukee in 1871. Within Illinois, the line was built by the Chicago, Milwaukee & St. Paul Railway (the name adopted by the entire St. Paul system in 1874). In the spring of 1873, the new railway, located several miles inland from the North Western, was completed to Western Avenue and Kinzie Street at the western boundary of Chicago.

To reach downtown, the St. Paul allied with the Panhandle, using the latter's circuitous line between Kinzie and Carroll Streets. From the Western Avenue junction switch eastward, the Panhandle sold the St. Paul a half interest in its properties. Having learned a hard lesson about the hazards of buildings made from wood, Chicago now required most structures to be made of fireproof materials, and an important source of traffic for the St. Paul was bricks for rebuilding the city. The railroad built three freight houses east of Halsted Street to distribute the bricks.

In 1874 the St. Paul contracted with the Panhandle, the Pennsylvania, and the Alton to build a unified station on Fort Wayne's property at Canal and Adams Streets. The nine-track Chicago Union Passenger Depot opened for business on April 4, 1882. The Burlington, unhappy with the trek across the St. Charles Air Line to reach the IC's lakefront terminal, began serving the new station on June 19 after completing connecting tracks at Canal and 16th Street.

Chicago & Iowa

Although C&NW component Galena & Chicago Union never reached Galena, Illinois Central got there in 1854. The G&CU remained content with an agreement to haul the IC's Chicago traffic via the junction between the two railroads at Freeport.

This changed when Francis E. Hinckley, a contractor specializing in bridges, agreed in 1867 to build a span over the Rock River at Oregon, Illinois. At Oregon, he met local entrepreneurs who wanted to build a fifteen-mile railroad east to Rochelle to connect with the North Western. Hinckley offered to help and assumed the presidency of the Ogle & Carroll County Railroad. However, he had a better business plan. By extending his little pike east to Aurora and west to a connection with IC at Forreston, Hinckley and the Burlington could take the IC's Chicago traffic away from the C&NW. CB&Q agreed, and the renamed Chicago & Iowa Railroad (C&I) opened its eighty-two-mile line on January 1, 1872. The town of Squaw Grove, on the new and busy railroad, renamed itself Hinckley in honor of the man.

Not everyone was impressed. C&I's English bondholders charged Hinckley with fraud, so in 1877 he put the railroad in receivership to escape them. Burlington took control in 1882 and opened an extension from Oregon to Savanna, where the C&I connected with the affiliated Chicago, Burlington & Northern Railroad to Minnesota's Twin Cities (completed by 1886). To this day, BNSF train crews and dispatchers refer to the Aurora–Savanna main line as the C&I.

Baltimore & Ohio Reaches Chicago

Baltimore & Ohio, formed in 1827, was known as the Mother of American Railroads and pioneered many industry innovations. B&O began as a link from its namesake seaport at Baltimore to the continent's inland waterways via the Ohio River port at Wheeling, Virginia (later West Virginia). After the Civil War, B&O president John Garrett embarked on an ambitious expansion, including a 263-mile Chicago extension.

The Baltimore, Pittsburgh & Chicago Railroad (later renamed the Baltimore & Ohio & Chicago—one of the few railroad names incorporating two ampersands) commenced building westward from Chicago Junction on B&O's Newark, New Jersey–Sandusky, Ohio, line in 1873. It reached Chicago in 1874, giving the B&O system a 795-mile route between the Atlantic Ocean and Chicago, which was notably shorter than competitors Pennsylvania (899 miles) and New York Central (980 miles).

To reach downtown Chicago, B&O&C built along the north side of the Lake Shore & Michigan Southern and Fort Wayne lines to 95th Street, where it met the South Chicago branch of the Rock Island. B&O&C then turned north for about a mile before vectoring northwest to a junction with the Illinois Central main line at Brookdale (69th Street), using IC to reach downtown. For its first passenger terminal, B&O&C occupied a portion of the post-fire Interstate Exposition Building between Madison and Jackson Streets, and it built a freight yard at South Chicago between 84th and 90th Streets.

Chicago & Pacific

The original St. Charles Air Line company had envisioned connecting Chicago with Savanna on the Mississippi River but never reached this goal, and as late as 1870, Savanna was still without a railway. A company ambitiously named Atlantic & Pacific Railroad—renamed Chicago & Pacific (C&P) in 1872—was incorporated to bridge that gap. To avoid the cost of building into downtown Chicago, C&P elected to begin laying track on Goose Island, an artificial island on Chicago's North Side resulting from construction of the Ogden Canal between bends in the North Branch of the Chicago River. C&P crossed the C&NW south of Clybourn (where the North Western's lines to Milwaukee and Janesville split) then

In 1882–1883, Belt Railway of Chicago (BRC) built northward to meet Milwaukee Road antecedent Chicago & Pacific at Cragin (junction at far left). In this view looking north, BRC's line is seen curving to the left meeting Canadian Pacific (CP) Railway's Elgin Subdivision (former Milwaukee Road/C&P route) and crossing Union Pacific's former C&NW Junction Line from 40th Street to Mayfair at the diamond called Cragin Crossing (at the center of the photo). Until the 1980s, the Junction Line continued north from Mayfair to Evanston. Since this 1990s photo, the UP diamonds at Cragin have been removed and the connection to CP rebuilt with double track. *Sean Graham-White*

Grand Trunk Western Pacific 5629 leads a fan trip at Chicago's Dearborn Station on October 29, 1966. Although not a major passenger carrier, GTW provided parent Canadian National with access to the Chicago market. GTW 5629 survived the mass scrapping at the end of the steam era and served as a popular excursion engine in the 1960s. Unfortunately, the privately held locomotive was scrapped at Blue Island in 1987 when its owner, Dick Jensen, became entangled in a dispute with Metra, on whose property the locomotive was stored. *J. Michael Gruber collection*

followed Bloomingdale Avenue to a crossing of the St. Paul line that today is still known as Pacific Junction (or Tower A5).

C&P's investors were allied with Delaware, Lackawanna & Western Railroad (DL&W), which planned to connect with it via Great Lakes boats sailing from DL&W's western terminus in Buffalo, New York. But DL&W bowed out of the picture when C&P's bondholders took control of the failing property in 1876. The line was sold to the St. Paul on April 1, 1880. Under St. Paul ownership, the C&P extended to Savanna and across the Mississippi to Sabula, Iowa.

Intertwined with C&P was the Chicago & Evanston Railroad (C&E), begun by street railway interests to link those lakefront cities. St. Paul acquired the C&E in 1887, integrating it into C&P's operations. A swing bridge across the North Branch at Kinzie Street connected the C&E/C&P with St. Paul's Chicago main line, providing downtown access.

Chicago's Only Narrow Gauge

In the early 1870s, narrow gauge fever crossed the Atlantic from Great Britain, and some 18,500 miles of mostly three-foot gauge track were built in North America. On December 5, 1872, the Chicago, Millington & Western Railway was formed to build a three-foot gauge line from Chicago through Warrenville, Millington, Princeton, and Neponset to Muscatine, Iowa, parallel with the Burlington. By 1875, eleven miles of track had been laid from 22nd and Ashland in Chicago along Blue Island Avenue and 26th Street to gravel pits in what later was developed as Westchester. However, the diminuitive line couldn't pay its construction debt and ended operations in 1877, just a year after they began. Burlington bought the property in 1879 and abandoned most of it, though it retained (and standard-gauged) a mile or so of track along Blue Island Avenue.

The Grand Trunk Western

Supported by the British and Canadian governments, the Grand Trunk Railway (GT) was incorporated in 1852 to link the Atlantic port at Portland, Maine, with the Canadian and American interior. The line later focused on Chicago as its western terminus. In its early years, GT cooperated with established trans-Michigan railroads, connecting with them by building the sixty-mile Chicago, Detroit & Canada Grand Trunk Junction Railroad from Port Huron to Detroit (completed in 1859). It was on this railway that twelve-year-old Thomas Edison got his start, selling newspapers and candy to the passengers and conducting chemistry experiments in the railroad's baggage car during layovers.

After Michigan Central became part of the Vanderbilt empire in 1878, it raised its rates in an effort to divert GT's long-distance traffic to the NYC system. GT reacted in 1879 by buying a chain of short lines between Port Huron and Valparaiso and building its own track from Valparaiso to Thornton Junction, Illinois. It also acquired the Chicago & Southern, originally intended as the northernmost segment of the Chicago & Eastern Illinois, for the final few miles into Chicago. Through service between Port Huron and Chicago began on February 8, 1880, and the various American properties were consolidated as the Chicago & Grand Trunk Railway that year, then reorganized as the Grand Trunk Western (GTW) in 1900. Canadian National Railway was created in 1919 to take over the Grand Trunk system and other failing Canadian carriers, and GTW has been part of the CN system ever since.

Chicago & Western Indiana Provides Chicago Access for Chicago & Eastern Illinois, Grand Trunk, Erie, Monon, and Wabash

With an improving economy in the late 1870s, many new railroads wanted to enter Chicago but were deterred by the rising costs of downtown real estate and political hostility due to noise, smoke, and congestion complaints. John B. Brown, a promoter with

South of Dearborn Station on July 16, 1958, Chicago & Eastern Illinois NW2 switcher 121 works local freight at 15th Street. Notice the crossing tender's shack between tracks. C&EI was one of several late-entry roads that used Chicago & Western Indiana's line to reach downtown Chicago, after the Panic of 1873 derailed its original plan to enter the city over what later became the Grand Trunk Western. *Richard Jay Solomon*

Erie Railroad was the weakest of the four major east-west trunks connecting the New York City metropolitan area with Chicago. Its western connection reached the Chicago terminal area by 1882. Although it operated less frequent passenger service than NYC or PRR, with its Chicago trains serving Dearborn Station, Erie was a substantial freight hauler. Erie merged with Delaware, Lackawanna & Western in 1960, forming Erie Lackawanna Railway (EL), and EL was blended into Conrail in 1976. Passenger service ended in 1970, and very little of Erie's Chicago extension survives today. *J. Michael Gruber collection*

a solution, founded the Chicago & Western Indiana Railroad (C&WI) on June 5, 1879, to provide Chicago access and terminal facilities for these new railroad competitors. C&WI's early support came from the Chicago & Eastern Illinois, stuck at its connection with the Panhandle at Dolton and eager to extend downtown. To spread the costs, C&EI recruited the Grand Trunk and three other expanding carriers to invest in the C&WI, which these five lines bought from Brown in 1882.

The Erie system was a group of affiliated broad gauge railroads extending west from Jersey City, New Jersey (opposite the Hudson River from New York City) to Marion, Ohio, where the route turned southwest toward Cincinnati. Chicago & Atlantic Railway

(C&A) had been organized on June 19, 1873, to build a connection from the Erie at Marion to Chicago. Paradoxically, although Erie tracks were six-foot gauge, the C&A opted for three-foot gauge and built nine miles of narrow gauge track between Huntington and Markle, Indiana, before Erie acquired the property in November 1880. Having just regauged its system to standard in 1879, the Erie wasn't interested in a slim gauge route and converted the C&A (later renamed Chicago & Erie) to standard gauge in 1881. By December 9, 1882, this company had finished a well-engineered line to Hammond, Indiana.

Another narrow gauge project was the Indianapolis, Delphi & Chicago Railroad (ID&C), incorporated on June 28, 1865.

Left: At Hammond Yard (HY) Tower in Hammond, the tower operator is giving a highball to a westbound EL freight train in February 1976. Erie/EL and Monon shared a passenger station in downtown Hammond. Chesapeake & Ohio of Indiana operated over these tracks after forsaking the Hammond Belt Railway connection with Indiana Harbor Belt in what's now Calumet City, Illinois. *Don Ellison;* **Right:** An eastbound Erie Lackawanna freight led by GP35 2568 slams across Indiana Harbor Belt's line to Burnham Yard, as viewed from Chicago & Western Indiana's 1897 State Line Tower in June 1974. In the background a Norfolk & Western switch engine can be seen on the former Nickel Plate. State Line was one of the largest mechanical interlockings in the Chicago area, as evidenced by the multitude of rods to the right of the tower. Still ahead of the EL train is the crossing of B&O Chicago Terminal's double track line on the south side of the tower. *Don Ellison;* **Below:** In May 1968, a quartet of Alco C420s lead a Monon freight from Louisville northward at Hammond, Indiana. The train is crossing the Little Calumet River and is approaching the south end of Monon's Hammond Yard. Hammond was Monon's base for Chicago-area freight operations, and it featured a ten-stall roundhouse at its south end. Monon focused second-generation diesel purchases on Alco. Many of its C420s, bought after much larger C628s broke too many rails, would continue to work for Louisville & Nashville (L&N) after L&N acquired the line in 1971. *Terry Norton*

This property drew the attention of the Chicago & South Atlantic Railroad, which planned to incorporate the ID&C in a proposed main line from downtown Chicago to Charleston, South Carolina. Although eighty miles of ID&C roadbed were graded, the project collapsed during the Panic of 1873, ultimately leaving a three-foot gauge road from Delphi to Rensselaer, Indiana. In 1881 this company, by then renamed Chicago & Indianapolis Air Line Railway, passed into the hands of the Louisville, New Albany & Chicago Railroad (which evolved into the Monon). The Air Line, converted to standard gauge, completed a connection with the Panhandle near Dyer (now Munster), Indiana, on August 22, 1881. By 1884 it had extended to Hammond to join the Erie line.

Another of C&WI's tenants was the Wabash. In 1879 Jay Gould acquired control of several railroads that he merged into the Wabash, St. Louis & Pacific Railway, extending from Toledo to Kansas City, Missouri. Gould's investments in the Union Pacific and Missouri Pacific set off a territorial war with Burlington, which resulted in Gould extending the Wabash to Chicago.

In 1872, Francis E. Hinckley, fresh from his work on the Chicago & Iowa, commenced construction of a line called the Chicago & Paducah Railroad (C&P) that was hoping to connect Streator, Illinois, with the Ohio River. This project stalled in 1874, and on May 1, 1879, Hinckley sold the route to Gould's Wabash (which crossed C&P at Bement, Illinois). Wabash built the Chicago & Strawn Railway to complete its route to Auburn Park Junction in Chicago. In 1893 the Wabash would add an eastward line from Chicago, known as the Pumpkin Vine, that stretched across northern Indiana to a connection with the railroad's east-west main at Montpelier, Ohio. Wabash was unique among Chicago's railroads because it operated trackage both east and west of the city.

Two of Chicago's minor passenger players were Wabash and Grand Trunk Western, both of which served Dearborn Street Station via Chicago & Western Indiana. John Gruber exposed this view of an outbound Wabash train from a GTW excursion in the mid-1960s. *John Gruber*

Chicago & Eastern Illinois and Rock Island were among the railroads that bought the passenger service version of EMD's F7, designated the FP7A. Locomotives from both roads meet near 16th Street, where Chicago & Western Indiana's route to Dearborn Street ducked under other lines. At the time of this photo C&EI served Dearborn, and Rock Island served LaSalle Street. However, between 1904 and 1913 C&EI, then under common control with the Rock Island, terminated its trains at LaSalle Street Station. *Richard Jay Solomon*

Chicago & Western Indiana (C&WI) was built in phases. Its main line extended south from downtown to reach the Wabash at Auburn Park Junction and the C&EI at Dolton. A branch, the South Chicago & Western Indiana, diverged at 79th Street and wended around the east side of Lake Calumet to Hammond, where it met the Chicago & Erie and the Louisville, New Albany & Chicago. In 1883, Chicago authorized construction of C&WI's large downtown passenger terminal, Dearborn Station, at Dearborn and Polk Streets, which was completed in 1885. The Grand Trunk built a connecting line (the Grand Trunk Junction Railway) along 49th Street from Elsdon to the C&WI main to bring its trains into Dearborn.

Belt Railway of Chicago

By the 1880s the volume of freight traffic moving through Chicago demanded additional track capacity. Also, it made sense to move interchanges away from the congested and expensive downtown core. The most significant element of C&WI's Chicago terminal project was its Belt Division, built to connect its owners with other Chicago railroads.

C&WI's Belt Railway of Chicago (BRC) was incorporated November 22, 1882. It diverged from C&WI's main line at Auburn Park Junction and ran parallel with the Wabash westward to Cicero Avenue, where it turned north to reach a junction with the Chicago & Pacific at Cragin. BRC exercised trackage rights over C&WI to

Above: Southern Pacific's late-era access to the Chicago gateway, beginning in 1989, was short-lived, as Union Pacific absorbed SP in 1996, less than seven years later. In this July 1, 1995, photograph, new SP GE AC4400CWs rest at Clearing Yard among BN SD9s and secondhand Wisconsin & Southern EMD's. Wisconsin & Southern began serving Chicago when it acquired Wisconsin & Calumet in 1992, a line that had obtained trackage rights over Metra south of Fox Lake, Illinois in 1989. *Brian Solomon;*
Below: A sign encouraging railroad employees near the entrance to Belt Railway of Chicago's Clearing Yard. In its early years Clearing Yard suffered from a dearth of traffic, but today it is one of Chicago's busiest yards and served by most of the area's railroads. *Brian Solomon*

Pullman Junction and built extensive industrial lines in the Calumet region. Its L-shaped system opened on May 1, 1883, and connected with almost every railroad serving Chicago.

Separately, railroad promoter Alpheus Beede Stickney incorporated the Chicago Union Transfer Railway (CUT) in 1889 to build a gigantic freight terminal that would serve as an unified interchange point for all Chicago's railroads—effectively a freight car clearinghouse, thus Stickney's name for the terminal, Clearing Yard. Stickney planned an unorthodox radial pinwheel arrangement with four yards connected by a circular hub track, to be located just west of Cicero Avenue (in close proximity to the Belt). Elements of this bizarre facility were built, but when the Belt refused to interchange cars, Stickney's company ran out of money.

H. H. Porter, chairman of C&EI, revived the Clearing Yard project in 1898, this time rebuilding it for gravity-driven hump yard switching. Completed and opened on April 1, 1902, Porter's revamped Clearing Yard was the third hump yard opened in the United States. Despite the

Above: John Gruber made this atmospheric telephoto image of the sunset at Belt Railway of Chicago's Clearing Yard while illustrating Jerry Pinkepank's September 1965 article for *Trains*. Although more than a dozen of John's photos were included, this one did not make editor David P. Morgan's final cut. *John Gruber;* **Below:** A cropped version of this iconic silhouette of an EMD cow-calf transfer locomotive on the Clearing Hump appeared on the cover of September 1966 *Trains* magazine that featured Belt Railway of Chicago. The cow-calf was a semipermanently coupled switcher with cabless B-unit and designed for slow-speed high–tractive effort applications such as switching long cuts of cars and shoving them over humps. BRC was the last operator of such locomotives. *John Gruber*

improved productivity, Chicago railroads refused to pay for the added expense of classifying cars at Clearing, so the yard closed after just a month and lay idle for another decade.

In 1910, rising freight congestion virtually shut down the entire Chicago terminal area, an event that encouraged the line-haul railroads to embrace BRC, Clearing Yard, and other belt lines. Under a 1912 agreement, seven carriers joined the C&WI's owners in acquiring the CUT company and merging it with BRC. Clearing was reconfigured into a bidirectional hump yard, and a new bypass was constructed along 59th Street (between the yard's west end and BRC's north-south main) to handle additional traffic. BRC has remained a vital part of Chicago's freight infrastructure ever since.

BRC continued the steam-era practice of fitting its switchers with steel tires rather than turning to the more common one-piece wheels as a result of exceptional flange wear caused by tight curvature. In BRC's shop a tire is heated in a time-honored process that permitted its removal from the wheel. *John Gruber*

Nickel Plate Road

George I. Seney was a New York investor whose syndicate in 1880 controlled several railroads, including the Lake Erie & Western (LE&W), which ran between Fremont, Ohio, and Bloomington, Illinois. However, when Wabash and New York Central colluded to starve LE&W by routing traffic around it, Seney responded by expanding his system toward Chicago, Cleveland, and New York.

Seney acquired the right-of-way of the proposed Wabash & Erie Canal and the Continental Railway—a visionary 1,200-mile air line designed to connect New York City with Union Pacific at Omaha, which had failed during the Panic of 1873. His group incorporated the New York, Chicago & St. Louis Railroad on April 13, 1881, to build a Buffalo–Cleveland–Chicago railroad on this property.

The unusual nickname Nickel Plate Road (NKP) stemmed from a report in the Norwalk, Ohio, *Chronicle* of the arrival of surveyors employed by the "great New York and St. Louis double track, nickel plated railroad." Ironically, the company elected to build through neighboring Bellevue instead. But the Nickel Plate Road moniker stuck and became the railroad's trade name, appearing on timetables, advertising, and equipment.

Nickel Plate construction progressed rapidly, and within a year the main line had reached Chicago's outskirts at Hammond. The railroad allied with the Illinois Central and built through the swamps around Lake Calumet to reach the IC's main line at 83rd Street, then completed a parallel track to Grand Crossing on August 24, 1882. NKP's Chicago passenger service was inaugurated to IC's Great Central Station on October 23. This terminal arrangement lasted only briefly, as Nickel Plate trains soon moved to a temporary station at 14th Street owned by B&O.

Seney's Nickel Plate system from Buffalo to Cleveland to Chicago ran parallel (and often adjacent) to New York Central System's Lake Shore & Michigan Southern. William H. Vanderbilt was unhappy with the competition and worried the new road would sell itself to his archrival Gould. Thus, Vanderbilt's LS&MS bought a controlling interest in the Nickel Plate just three days after NKP's first passenger train steamed out of Chicago. On May 1, 1883, Nickel Plate shifted its passenger trains to Rock Island and LS&MS's Chicago terminal at Van Buren Street. Nickel Plate freight was classified at Fordham Yard, located immediately east of the IC main line.

Nickel Plate Road's *New Yorker* departs LaSalle Street Station behind a pair of the railroad's distinctively painted Alco PA diesels. Nickel Plate was only a minor player in the Chicago passenger scene. It was one of three railroads serving LaSalle Street Station at the time, a legacy of its control by NYC. LaSalle Street Station, which had opened on July 1, 1903, replaced the older Van Buren Street Station that was built after the 1871 fire. *Richard Jay Solomon*

Hinckley and the Santa Fe

Francis E. Hinckley's third significant railroad promotion was the Chicago, Pekin & South-Western (CP&SW), a line originally conceived by Pekin, Illinois, investors as a direct rail link from that town to Chicago. Hinckley took control in 1872, and by January 6, 1873, CP&SW had built 56.5 miles from Pekin northeast to Streator (where the line connected with the Ottawa, Oswego & Fox River Valley Railroad, a Burlington feeder). Though his railroad reached a junction with Alton's Chicago & Illinois River Railroad at Mazon on May 21, 1876, Hinckley's legal problems stemming from the Chicago & Iowa and a quarrel with the Alton resulted in CP&SW bankruptcy in 1877. On May 10, 1882, Hinckley reorganized the property as the Chicago, St. Louis & Western Railroad (later Chicago & St. Louis Railway [C&StL]) and extended it another 60.2 miles from Mazon through Joliet

to Crawford (now Pulaski) Avenue in Chicago. The 140-mile line, known as the Hinckley Road, opened on January 1, 1884.

By the 1880s, the Atchison, Topeka & Santa Fe Railroad (Santa Fe) had evolved into a 5,217-mile system reaching from Kansas City, Missouri, west to the Pacific Coast and south to Texas. In its early years, it interchanged eastward traffic at Kansas City, but in the 1880s Rock Island, Burlington, and Missouri Pacific expanded into the Great Plains. Santa Fe retaliated by acquiring the Chicago & St. Louis Railway on December 15, 1886, making Hinckley a Santa Fe officer and organizing an air line link from Ancona (west of Streator) to Kansas City. C&StL's original trackage was improved with line changes, heavier trestles, and forty-three miles of passing sidings. When the bridge over the Illinois River was completed on December 17, 1887, Santa Fe's new line through Illinois was ready for service.

To improve the Hinckley Road's rudimentary terminal facilities, Santa Fe bought Grand Trunk's ex-Chicago & Southern line north of Elsdon (49th Street) on July 20, 1887, while arranging to use that carrier's access to Dearborn Station. For freight, Santa Fe built Corwith Yard north of Elsdon along the Chicago & Southern alignment. (In 1902, Santa Fe leased the C&S track north of its main line to Illinois Northern Railway, an industrial railroad serving International Harvester's McCormick Reaper Works.)

Meanwhile, Illinois Central incorporated Chicago, Madison & Northern Railroad (CM&N) in 1886 to build a 112-mile route (including branches into Wisconsin) from Freeport to Chicago, bypassing CB&Q's Chicago & Iowa. Expensive Chicago real estate costs stalled CM&N at Elmhurst until IC and Santa Fe agreed to build a joint entry to Chicago

Above: Threading its way out of Corwith Yard, Santa Fe's QNYLA begins its 2,215-mile journey from Chicago to Los Angeles with a quartet of freshly repainted FP45s (a model Santa Fe designated SDFP45 after rebuilding). QNYLA served as the westward connection from Conrail's TVLA intermodal train that ran from Bergen, New Jersey, to Santa Fe's Corwith Yard. In 1989, Santa Fe revived the red and silver warbonnet livery, initially applying it to the FP45 fleet, and soon afterward to all new road locomotives, most of which were assigned to intermodal service. *Mike Abalos*; **Below:** In June 1961, Santa Fe EMD F3s lead an outbound passenger train from Dearborn underneath Rock Island's line (to LaSalle Street) near 16th Street. In the 1890s Santa Fe cooperated with Illinois Central in constructing a joint entry from roughly California Avenue across the South Branch of the Chicago River at Bridgeport and eastward to junctions at Stewart Avenue, where Santa Fe connected with Chicago & Western Indiana to reach Dearborn Station. Santa Fe served Dearborn until the eve of Amtrak on May 2, 1971. *Richard Jay Solomon*

On August 20, 1993, EMD/Siemens F69PH-ACs lead Amtrak's borrowed German ICE train westward on Santa Fe west of Bridgeport. In the background is Illinois Central's IMX ('Intermodal Exchange') facility, built in 1970 to replace IC's old piggyback ramp at Congress Street, which Southern Pacific was leasing at the time of the photograph. Santa Fe's line was the route for Amtrak's *Southwest Chief* out of Chicago until 1996, when it was shifted to former BN lines between Chicago and Cameron, Illinois. *Mike Abalos*

that shaved 4.12 miles off Santa Fe's route when it opened on November 18, 1891. A two-mile branch off the CM&N line to Addison, Illinois, hosted one of Chicago's most obscure suburban services between 1892 and 1931.

Chicago & Northern Pacific and Grand Central Station

Northern Pacific Railway (NP) spanned the northern tier of states and territories west from St. Paul and Duluth, Minnesota, reaching Portland, Oregon, in 1885 and Puget Sound in 1888. Seeking a connection to Chicago to complete its system, NP formed an alliance with the 486-mile Wisconsin Central Railroad.

WC owned lines from Portage and Neenah to Stevens Point, Wisconsin, and then to a Lake Superior port at Ashland. Initially, WC

depended on logging traffic, but as the forests became depleted, it viewed a linkup with NP as a profitable substitute. In 1885, WC extended to St. Paul to establish an NP connection. That move, though, caused friction with the Chicago, Milwaukee & St. Paul, on which WC depended to reach Milwaukee and Chicago. In 1886 WC built an independent link, the Chicago, Wisconsin & Minnesota Railroad, southward to Chicago from its St. Paul connection at Schlesingerville (now Slinger), Wisconsin, via Waukesha, Wisconsin, and Antioch, Wheeling, and Des Plaines, Illinois.

WC took control of the newly built Chicago & Great Western to secure Chicago terminal access from a junction at Central Avenue, and C&GW contracted with the Panhandle to reach the Union Stock Yards. In November 1887 WC leased the Chicago, Harlem & Batavia Railway (CH&B),

Above: In 1909, Minneapolis, St. Paul & Sault Ste. Marie (known as the 'Soo Line') gained access to Chicago by leasing the original Wisconsin Central. Soo was largely a freight hauler. On April 11, 1942, Soo Line's Alco-built 4-8-2 4012 works a transfer freight on BRC at 63rd street near Harlem Avenue. *J. Michael Gruber collection;* **Right:** Chicago, St. Paul & Kansas City Railroad was reorganized as the Chicago Great Western in 1892. Although CGW offered connections to important gateways at Kansas City, Minneapolis–St. Paul, and Omaha, its route structure was circuitous, and it remained a relatively minor Chicago player. In this classic urban steam-era scene, a CGW 0-6-0 drills boxcars. *J. Michael Gruber collection*

known as the Dummy Line, which operated suburban passenger service on a route parallel to Madison Avenue from Crawford (now Pulaski) Avenue to Forest Park. NP and WC cemented their relationship with a traffic agreement in 1889 and a ninety-nine-year lease of WC by NP in 1890. On March 11, 1890, NP formed Chicago & Northern Pacific Railroad (C&NP) to amalgamate C&GW and CH&B. Work was already proceeding on the C&NP's signature development, Grand Central Station at the corner of Harrison and Fifth (now Wells) Streets, which opened later that year. (See Chapter 2.)

Meanwhile, the Minnesota & Northwestern, led by Stickney (later the

promoter of Clearing Yard), acquired the rights to the old St. Charles Air Line right-of-way through DuPage and western Cook Counties, and made an agreement with C&GW for terminal facilities. It opened its route from Oelwein, Iowa, to Chicago on August 1, 1887. The company was sold to the Chicago, St. Paul & Kansas City Railroad in December 1887, and reorganized as the Chicago Great Western (CGW) in 1892.

Right: On March 22, 1942, Chicago Great Western crews are rerailing derailed 2-8-2 701 at Villa Park, Illinois. Like most American railroads, CGW phased out steam after World War II; it bought diesels largely from Electro-Motive, and it favored F-units for road work. *J. Michael Gruber collection*;
Below: Among Chicago Great Western's last new steam locos were "super power" 2-10-4 Texas types. CGW received two orders from Baldwin in 1930 and one order from Lima in 1931. On February 22, 1943, Baldwin-built CGW 871 leads a westward freight over the pin-connected deck truss spanning the Fox River at St. Charles, Illinois. Although much of the CGW route was abandoned after inclusion in Chicago & North Western, this portion of its line over the Fox River wasn't lifted until September 2013. *J. Michael Gruber collection*

Elgin, Joliet & Eastern

Philip B. Shumway, who had worked with Francis Hinckley on the Chicago, Pekin & South-Western, dreamed of an outer belt line around the Chicago terminal. In 1886 he bought and rapidly completed the twenty-two-mile Joliet, Aurora & Northern Railway (JA&N), but couldn't afford to complete his envisioned Chicago ring.

Alex Leith, a vice president of the Joliet Iron and Steel Company, embraced Shumway's belt line and is believed to have convinced the steel firm's banker, Drexel Morgan & Company of New York, to finance the project. J. Pierpont Morgan took control, incorporated the Elgin, Joliet & Eastern Railway (EJ&E) on March 18, 1887, and hired Shumway to build the line from Elgin (on the Chicago & Pacific) around Chicago to Valparaiso. Sadly, Shumway died less than two months later, and Morgan brought in New York contractor F. E. Worcester to complete the job.

Under Worcester EJ&E extended by 1888 from Spaulding (a junction with Chicago,

Milwaukee & St. Paul east of Elgin), to Normantown on the JA&N, and from Joliet to McCool, Indiana (junction with the Baltimore & Ohio). A connecting line, the Gardner, Coal City & Northern, diverged at Walker (Plainfield) into the Grundy County coalfields near Coal City, Illinois. An extension was built the following year as the Waukegan & Southwestern Railway from Spaulding to Waukegan (a Lake Michigan port north of Chicago) to carry iron ore to Leith's Joliet works. In 1893 EJ&E lengthened its eastern leg from McCool to Porter, Indiana, to connect with the Lake Shore & Michigan Southern, completing its steel arc around Chicago.

Joliet Steel was owned by Illinois Steel, which operated steel mills on Chicago's North Side (the North Works) and South Side (the South Works, on the lakefront between 79th Street and the Calumet River). Illinois Steel's plant railroad, the Calumet & Blue Island, struck a deal with Chicago & Eastern Illinois in 1893 to operate trains to coalfields near Danville, Illinois (which lasted until 1947). In 1895–1896, an affiliated railroad called

EJ&E SD38-2s 660 and 670 cross the Des Plaines River in Libertyville, Illinois, en route to Joliet from Waukegan on November 19, 2003. In its later years, the Indiana end of the railroad saw the most action, while the north end hosted only one to two trains daily. Since acquisition by Canadian National in 2009, the north end of the railroad has become much busier west (railroad east) of the connection with the former Wisconsin Central at Leithton. *Terry Norton*

Above: Elgin, Joliet & Eastern took an unusual approach toward dieselization. In 1946, it was first to order a Baldwin center-cab locomotive (model DT-6-6-2000) rated at 2,000 horsepower. This unit, powered by a pair of 1,000-horsepower 608NA engines, was designed for high tractive effort and slow speed freight service. Based on its success, EJ&E ordered a fleet of similar center cabs, powered by pairs of turbocharged 606SC engines. Difficulties with the Baldwin diesel engines led EJ&E to re-engine some of them with more reliable EMD prime movers. A pair of re-engined center cabs work at Leithton in May 1964. *Terry Norton;*
Bottom Right: Just eighteen days after the Elgin, Joilet & Eastern Railway was officially acquired by the CN Rail system, things haven't changed; EJ&E SW1001 446 and crew have just made an interchange move at the Chicago Short Line interlocking in South Chicago, on Feb. 19, 2009. This is the Lakefront Transfer operating on the former EJ&E Lake Front Line that extends from Kirk Yard in Gary, Indiana. *Eric Powell*

Chicago, Lake Shore & Eastern constructed a 10.5-mile lakefront line from South Works to a connection with B&O and LS&MS at Clarke Junction (now Gary), Indiana. Illinois Steel acquired EJ&E in 1898, and in 1900 built the Griffith & Northern between Griffith and East Chicago, Indiana, to connect the EJ&E with CLS&E. (EJ&E leased CLS&E in 1909.)

In 1901, bankers at the House of Morgan created United States Steel (USS) by facilitating a combination of Illinois Steel with Andrew Carnegie's steelmaking assets. The new company built Gary Works, named for USS's first president, on the sand dunes at the southernmost tip of Lake Michigan, beginning production in 1908. EJ&E was the only railroad serving the Gary Works; voluminous shipments of coal and limestone inbound and steel products outbound made EJ&E a busy and profitable line. Popularly known as the J, EJ&E also promoted itself as Chicago's Outer Belt Line and was capable of transferring shipments between any pair of railroads serving the city.

The World's Columbian Exposition and the Wandering B&O

Chicago businessmen promoted a world's fair to be held in 1892 to mark the four hundredth anniversary of the first voyage of Christopher Columbus and to celebrate Chicago's rise from the ruins of the 1871 fire. Other cities, notably New York, also sought a Columbus-concept exposition, but Congress awarded the fair to Chicago in 1890. Sparing no expense, the World's Columbian Exposition hired Frederick Law Olmsted, designer of New York's Central Park, to lay out the fairgrounds in Jackson Park south of 57th Street on the lakefront, with the architectural firm of Daniel Burnham and John Wellmore Root overseeing design of exhibition halls. The project, which involved the construction of about two hundred buildings on 633 acres around an artificial lagoon, proved so ambitious it couldn't be completed in 1892, but President Grover Cleveland was on hand to press the button energizing the electric lights and motors in the White City on May 1, 1893.

Jackson Park's fairgrounds were close to the Illinois Central, and in preparation for the fair the IC undertook improvements, most notably the construction of a new Central Station at 12th Street (now Roosevelt Road) and the lakefront. By the 1890s, IC's Great Central Station near the Chicago River was completely overtaxed by through and suburban passenger volume, in addition to patrons of

Why would a Big Four engine be leading a train to Union Station? Under normal circumstances NYC's Big Four passenger trains served IC's Central Station (rather than LaSalle Street, which was the terminal for NYC trains running via the Lake Shore & Michigan Southern route). Might this be some sort of extra train or a World War II era-diversion? Perhaps another railroad borrowed the Big Four locomotive? *Photographer unknown, Solomon collection*

Illinois Central operated Chicago's oldest and most intensive suburban passenger service. Until electrification was completed in 1926, trains were steam-hauled using specialized bi-directional locomotives. Many were small Forney type engines, such as 2-4-4T number 1415. By the 1920s, this relic of an earlier age had worked for more than four decades hauling passengers. Its electric replacements had equally long careers. *John A. Rehor collection, Solomon archive*

the Michigan Central and the Cleveland, Columbus, Cincinnati & Indianapolis Railway (later the Cleveland, Cincinnati, Chicago & St. Louis Railway), known as the Big Four. The Big Four's predecessor reached a connection with IC at Kankakee, Illinois, in 1873, and IC began operating the Big Four's Indianapolis and Cincinnati through trains between Kankakee and Chicago in 1886.

During the fair's six-month run, the IC operated an average of 220 daily trains to the temporary passenger terminal inside the fairgrounds; this was in addition to more than 200 regular suburban trains. With the average fair train running nine to ten cars, on October 9, 1893, IC set a record by carrying 541,312 passengers within Chicago. Both Baltimore & Ohio and (by way of trackage rights) Chicago & Northern Pacific also ran trains to the fairgrounds.

In preparation for the fair, IC elevated its main line between 47th and 70th Streets to separate the heavy train traffic from hordes of pedestrians walking between the fairgrounds east of the tracks and the amusement park on the Midway to the west. However, the elevation broke the connection with the B&O at Brookdale. B&O was already looking for different terminal facilities, and the new Grand Central Station provided a solution—even though its approach tracks faced westward while B&O entered the city from the southeast. Initially, B&O reached Grand Central from 95th Street and the lakefront over the Rock Island's South Chicago branch (built in the early 1870s) and Suburban Line (relocated along 89th Street in 1890), the Panhandle and station owner Chicago & Northern Pacific. The first B&O trains appeared at Grand Central on December 1, 1891.

George M. Pullman and His Legacy

George Mortimer Pullman migrated west to Chicago in 1857, where he participated in the massive effort to raise downtown buildings from the original swampy grade level of the city. According to legend, after an excruciating overnight train ride, he turned his attention to making rail travel more comfortable. His first effort was converting two coaches to sleepers with twenty berths each, which went into service on the Alton in 1859. Pullman became famous in 1865 when his sleeping car *Pioneer* was switched into the train conveying the body of assassinated President Abraham Lincoln from Washington, D.C., to Springfield, Illinois.

Two years later, Pullman formed the Pullman Palace Car Company to build sleeping, dining, and other first-class passenger cars. Although Pullman had many competitors, his company prospered because of its reputation for high-quality accommodations and excellent service. Initially, Pullman manufacturing was centered in Detroit, but in 1880 the company relocated to a four-hundred-acre site south of Chicago along the Illinois Central main line near Lake Calumet. Pullman built a company town, named after himself, where workers could enjoy good jobs, good homes, and a wholesome atmosphere.

The model Pullman community was a popular side trip for fairgoers visiting Chicago's World's Columbian Exposition in 1893. However, a severe depression that year reduced sleeping car orders, inducing Pullman to cut wages to his seven thousand employees. Conversely, rents and store prices in Pullman were not reduced, because Pullman expected his investment in the town to remain profitable.

Pullman's squeeze on his workers gave the American Railway Union (ARU) an opening to organize thousands of Pullman employees. When attempts to negotiate with the company were rebuffed, the workers called a strike for May 11, 1894. To increase pressure on Pullman, on June 26 ARU asked its railroad members not

View from the fireman's side of a brand new Belt Railway of Chicago Alco C424 running long hood first as it approaches Pullman Junction in 1965. Named for the Pullman Railroad, which connected here, Pullman Junction was the crossing of the east-west Rock Island and BRC South Chicago branches with the Chicago & Western Indiana and the Nickel Plate. All trains were required to stop before proceeding through the junction, which was controlled by a C&WI operator. The highball signal in front of the semaphores governed train movements at the junction: diagonal meant proceed, any other position meant stop. *John Gruber*

to work on any train that carried Pullman cars. Long-distance rail travel across the Midwest and parts of the West ground to a halt.

The railroads hired strikebreakers, which enraged the strikers and resulted in violent clashes. Thirty died, fifty-seven were wounded, and property damage was estimated at more than $80 million. President Grover Cleveland ordered his attorney general to obtain an injunction against the strike, on the grounds that it interfered with transportation of the U.S. mail. When the ARU ignored the court's July 2 injunction, the federal government deployed ten thousand troops to enforce it. Railroad operations slowly returned to normal after the ARU withdrew its boycott on August 2, and Pullman's workers ended their strike in September.

A federal study commissioned by Cleveland criticized Pullman's "un-American" paternalism, and in 1898 the Illinois Supreme Court forced the company to divest the town because real estate operations weren't authorized by the corporate charter. Pullman himself suffered a fatal heart attack in 1897. Despite these setbacks, Pullman's company continued to dominate the manufacturing and operation of sleeping cars until 1944, when it was ordered by a federal court to divest one of the two businesses. Pullman continued to operate sleepers until December 31, 1968, when the cars were turned back to the railroads. Pullman-Standard, Pullman's car manufacturing arm, eventually was sold to Canada's Bombardier and Trinity Industries, which assumed its passenger and freight car designs, respectively. One of Pullman's last passenger car orders, manufactured at Hammond, was Amtrak's initial run of 284 Superliners in the late 1970s.

Today Pullman's town is a historic site owned by the State of Illinois. (See Chapter 2.) Pullman had its own railroad, which extended seventeen miles from Pullman Junction (near 95th Street and Stony Island) around the west side of Lake Calumet to 126th Street. Rock Island bought this line in 1949, which passed to Norfolk & Western following Rock's demise in 1980. It is now owned by Norfolk Southern, with Chicago Rail Link exercising trackage rights.

Horsecars, Cable Cars, Streetcars and the L

Chicago embraced mass transit in 1856, when it granted franchises to lay light rails in its muddy streets for horse-powered streetcars. By 1872, 188 horsecars worked the routes of the Chicago City Railway (CCRy), Chicago West Division Railway, and North Chicago City Railway.

In 1880, a director of the Chicago City Railway searching for cleaner and more efficient transport traveled to San Francisco to investigate the cable propulsion system pioneered there. His favorable reaction led to Chicago embracing cable car technology. In 1882 CCRy's first cable car lines opened on State Street and Wabash–Cottage Grove. By 1887 the Cottage Grove line was carrying up to one hundred thousand passengers per day in three-car trains. CCRy extended this line to 71st Street by 1890. At 8.7 miles, this was the longest cable car line ever built, taking about sixty-three minutes to ride from end to end.

The North Chicago and West Chicago Street Railroads, under the control of financier Charles T. Yerkes, began converting horsecar routes to cable propulsion in 1888 and 1890, respectively. Tunnels at LaSalle, Washington, and Van Buren Streets conveyed the cars under the busy Chicago River. Ultimately, Chicago possessed the longest cable car system ever built—eighty-two route-miles, operating 710 grip cars. Chicago's downtown Loop owes its name to the cable car loops built there.

By the mid-1890s, electric streetcar technology had proven a more economical transport solution, and in 1893 Chicago's street railways began converting their remaining horsecar lines to electric power. Cable car lines continued for another decade, in part due to political aversion to wires over downtown streets, but electric trolleys finally displaced the last cable cars working the Cottage Grove line on October 21, 1906. Although little remains of Chicago's cable car era, a CCRy grip car is preserved at the Museum of Science and Industry (located in the last surviving structure from the World's Columbian Exhibition).

During an afternoon deluge, C&NW Pacific 503 marches beneath the Lake Street L as a CTA electric train rumbles overhead. Notice the passengers riding on the open platform cars, traveling fearlessly despite the rain. The earliest Chicago Ls began as steam-powered lines but later adopted the third rail power distribution system successfully employed by the pioneering fairgrounds transit railway at the 1893 fair. *Philip A. Weibler*

North Chicago's powerhouse at LaSalle and Illinois Streets has housed a succession of restaurants.

The electric streetcar network was extensive. It blanketed Chicago's streets with more than a thousand miles of track, which extended beyond city limits into bordering suburbs and as far as Indiana. However, the Chicago Union Traction Company (reorganized in 1908 as the Chicago Railways) was financially troubled, and in 1914 the city consolidated Chicago Railways, CCRy, and two smaller companies as Chicago Surface Lines (CSL)—the world's largest streetcar system. Though CSL's red and cream cars fanned out into new residential neighborhoods as lines were extended throughout the 1920s, the advent of the automobile and the Great Depression devastated ridership and revenue, and by 1930 CSL's underlying private companies were in receivership. Meanwhile, CSL began experimenting with buses in 1927, and increasingly opted to initiate new routes with buses instead of streetcars.

In New York, elevated passenger railways had been developed to speed up city travel, and in 1888 the Chicago & South Side Rapid Transit was incorporated to bring that concept westward. Known as the Alley L—Chicago's elevated lines are called the L, and New York's are the El—the South Side line rode a steel superstructure behind houses and apartments, providing momentary glimpses into residents' private lives. The Alley L reached 39th Street in 1892 and extended to Jackson Park at 63rd Street on May 12, 1893, days after the World's Columbian Exposition opened.

The Lake Street L, from Madison and Market (now Wacker) to Lake Street and then west, opened November 1893; the Metropolitan West Side L, operating three branches, commenced in May 1895. Transit magnate Yerkes' Northwestern Elevated Railroad began operating at the end of 1899 (and was eventually extended to Evanston in 1908 over the Chicago & Evanston). Yerkes also bought the Lake Street L after it failed financially. Significantly, Yerkes promoted

North Shore's southbound *Electroliner* traverses the Chicago Loop approaching Randolph and Wells Station. Until January 1963, North Shore provided a swift and convenient downtown-to-downtown service between Chicago and Milwaukee. After North Shore ended operation, its *Electroliners* were sent to Philadelphia's Red Arrow Lines, where they operated as *Libertyliners. Richard Jay Solomon*

construction of a Union Loop L to unify the elevated lines downtown, overcoming opposition from downtown property owners who must have been apoplectic at the prospect of L trains roaring noisily overhead. Yerkes built the Lake Street leg of the Loop in 1894–1895 under the guise of an extension of the Lake L, but he had to pay off unhappy property owners to build tracks over Fifth (now Wells) and Wabash. The Van Buren segment was completed last, and the Loop began carrying revenue passengers on October 3, 1897. In later years, the Loop became instrumental in allowing through operation of L trains from one route to another, as well as efficiently distributing riders downtown.

Yerkes was reviled by Chicago's newspapers for allegedly hardhearted business practices and allegations of bribery and corruption, and he moved on to London to focus on expansion of London's Underground railway system. Samuel Insull, head of Chicago's electric utility, Commonwealth Edison, took over after Yerkes' departure. From 1911, Insull and his partners

A Chicago Transit Authority L train of 6000-class cars rebuilt from retired President's Conference Committee (PCC) streetcars is headed from Jackson Park to Howard Street. CTA and predecessor Chicago Surface Lines bought PCC streetcars, then between 1954 and 1959, CTA contracted with St. Louis Car to rebuild some 571 of these cars into rapid transit cars as streetcar service was converted to buses. *Richard Jay Solomon*

bought control of the L lines and operated them as a single system, merging them into the Chicago Rapid Transit Company in 1924. Under Insull's stewardship, the L was extended and improved, but the Depression unraveled Insull's industrial empire.

In 1945, the state legislature created the Chicago Transit Authority to acquire the L and surface streetcar lines, which took place in 1947. CTA replaced streetcars with buses, with the final trolleys traversing the Wentworth line on June 21, 1958. The L network was restructured by abandoning little-used branches and stations while building two new subways to supplement the Loop. Federal funds paid for the State Street subway under downtown (completed in 1943); the Dearborn Street subway was finished in 1958. The construction of expressways created new rights-of-way, and the West Side L was relocated to the median of the Congress Street (now Eisenhower) Expressway, opening that same year. The success of that arrangement led to L extensions down the medians of the Dan Ryan Expressway to 95th Street in 1969

and the Kennedy Expressway to Jefferson Park in 1970; in 1984 the latter line reached O'Hare Airport. A new route following railroad rights-of-way from the Loop to Midway Airport completed the current L system in 1993.

Indiana Harbor Belt and B&OCT

Indiana Harbor Belt (IHB), Chicago's busiest belt line, began as an effort to link industries in northwest Indiana, including Standard Oil's Whiting Refinery, with trunk lines west of Chicago. IHB predecessor Chicago, Hammond & Western Railroad (backed by meatpacker G. H. Hammond & Company) was chartered on April 21, 1896, to build around the south and west sides of Chicago to the St. Paul's Chicago & Pacific line, and it acquired the Hammond & Blue Island Railroad, which ran fourteen miles from Whiting to Blue Island with intentions of continuing northwestward from there.

Previously, the Chicago & Northern Pacific had extended its system, in 1891–1892, using its Chicago Central Railway (CC) to construct a link from C&NP's line at 14th and Western Streets southward to a connection with Chicago & Calumet Terminal Railroad (C&CT) at Blue Island. Belt Railway of Chicago allowed the CC to cross its trackage at 75th Street (Forest Hill) in exchange for local service rights over C&NP's Chicago & Southwestern Railroad subsidiary (which served a developing industrial area along 16th Street in Cicero). When Baltimore & Ohio shifted its Grand Central–bound passenger trains off the Panhandle route onto CC's line, it built the Baltimore & Ohio Connecting Railroad alongside the Panhandle to bridge the gap between 75th Street (Forest Hill) and the Rock Island connection near 90th and Paulina.

Northern Pacific failed in the 1893 depression, relinquishing control of both Wisconsin Central and C&NP. After four difficult years, C&NP was reorganized as the Chicago Terminal Transfer Railroad (CTTR). CTTR acquired Chicago & Calumet Terminal, a company that had been allied with B&O since 1887, in June 1898. To handle B&O's

To casual visitors, Chicago's subways aren't as obvious as the famous elevated routes, but the subways carry millions of passengers each year. The State Street subway was completed during World War II, but the parallel Dearborn Street Subway wasn't finished for another fifteen years. This 1994 view of the Dearborn Street subway shows Clark and Lake Station where passengers can connect with trains on the Loop. *Brian Solomon*

On July 18, 1958, Richard J. Solomon was given a private tour of Indiana Harbor Belt's Blue Island Yard at Riverdale, Illinois. IHB's western segment (jointly operated with Baltimore & Ohio Chicago Terminal) runs from Franklin Park (just east of Canadian Pacific's former Milwaukee Road Bensenville Yard) southeastward through Broadview, La Grange, Chicago Ridge, and Blue Island, where IHB operates a large classification yard. From here IHB's main line turns eastward through Riverdale, Dolton, and Burnham before arriving at Gibson Yard in Hammond, Indiana. IHB also operates over the former Chicago, Indiana & Southern, running north-south from the east end of Gibson Yard through East Chicago to a connection at CP 502 with the former New York Central Water Level Route (now Norfolk Southern's Chicago Line). *Richard Jay Solomon*

terminal traffic, C&CT had built a belt line from Whiting, Indiana, through Blue Island to a connection with the Santa Fe at McCook, and planned to expand northward.

Thus, by the mid-1890s, two terminal railroads were poised to build competing belt lines from Blue Island northwest. That didn't happen, though, because on October 5, 1896, Chicago, Hammond & Western and Chicago & Calumet Terminal agreed to create a joint belt line shared by both companies, an arrangement that has endured for a more than a century. C&CT constructed and owned track from Blue Island to Superior (near La Grange) while CH&W built from there to a connection with the St. Paul route at Franklin Park (reaching there in 1897). Each company had full rights

to switch any industry track connecting to the joint line. Also in 1897, the Terminal Railroad (affiliated with CH&W) built a line from Argo (Summit) eastward to the Stock Yards.

In 1901, CTTR extended northeastward from the end of the joint line at Franklin Park to a junction at Mayfair (on Chicago's North Side where Chicago & North Western and St. Paul lines crossed). This Mayfair extension was intended to attract traffic away from the Elgin, Joliet & Eastern, but that business didn't develop. CTTR never operated the Mayfair line, and it was abandoned around World War I.

In 1910, B&O bought the struggling CTTR's stock and changed its name to Baltimore & Ohio Chicago Terminal (B&OCT). Meanwhile, the New York Central system, through its Lake Shore & Michigan Southern and Michigan Central subsidiaries, had invested in the Chicago, Hammond & Western. Through a complicated reorganization on October 31, 1907, NYC created the Indiana Harbor Belt Railroad by combining CH&W, Terminal, and several small switching lines. Minority shares in IHB were sold to the St. Paul and Chicago & North Western in 1911 (C&NW sold its interest in 1961).

Responding to regulatory prodding from the state of Illinois, Chicago's railroads reached an agreement with shippers to implement uniform switching charges in 1911. This made Chicago more attractive for industrial development and promoted the interests of all area railroads. As a result, IHB and B&OCT experienced a flood of new traffic.

To make efficient use of new belt lines, line-haul railroads moved their principal freight yards outward from the city toward the suburban crossings of IHB and B&OCT. Immediately west of its IHB crossing, C&NW built a small yard at Proviso (Melrose Park) in 1903 and steadily expanded that facility until it became the world's largest freight yard in 1930. Similarly, the St. Paul established Bensenville (originally Godfrey) Yard in 1916, while in 1926 Illinois Central completed Markham Yard. The two belts constructed their own major freight classification yards: IHB at Gibson (Hammond), Indiana and Blue Island (the first hump yard to use mechanical car retarders), and B&OCT at Barr Yard in Riverdale, completed in 1948.

This aerial view of Argo Crossing from the mid-1990s shows Baltimore & Ohio Chicago Terminal's double track line (running from bottom left to top right) crossing Illinois Central's former Alton, then the Chicago Sanitary & Ship canal on a heavy truss bridge. The diamond crossing (once labeled as GM&O Junction on the now-razed tower) is also known as CP Canal as a result of its proximity to the waterway. The joint B&OCT/IHB line is an important link for freight interchange and intersects key east-west main lines on its way northward to Franklin Park, where it meets Canadian National's former Wisconsin Central and CP Rail's Elgin Sub. *Sean Graham-White*

Chicago's Last New Lines: Pere Marquette; Chicago, Milwaukee & Gary; St. Paul and New York Central Coal Extensions; and Chesapeake & Ohio

The Pere Marquette Railway (PM) was a financially challenged system serving Michigan and Ontario. Its route toward Chicago was built in 1872 by Chicago & West Michigan Railway (C&WM), running from its hub at Grand Rapids south to New Buffalo and later LaCrosse, Indiana. C&WM served Central Station in Chicago by way of the Michigan Central, but PM reached Chicago directly in 1903 by constructing a 21.5-mile branch from New Buffalo to Porter, Indiana. PM obtained Lake Shore & Michigan Southern trackage rights from Porter to Clarke Junction and beyond to downtown Chicago via the Fort Wayne, using the Chicago Terminal Transfer Railroad to reach Grand Central Station. PM freights initially terminated at Tracy Yard (near 103rd and Western). Later, PM switched its freight to Rockwell Street Yard, leased from Belt Railway of Chicago, and rerouted its

In May 1968, Baltimore & Ohio Alco S-2 switcher 9041 leads a wooden-bodied caboose eastbound in Hammond, Indiana. State Line Tower and the Illinois-Indiana border are five blocks to the west of here. Notice the elevated grade crossing tender's shack protecting Hohman Avenue. *Terry Norton*

passenger trains on the same route as B&O's from 95th Street to Grand Central Station.

EJ&E's success and the rise of the Gary Works encouraged a scheme for another circumferential outer belt beyond EJ&E's route. The Illinois, Indiana & Minnesota Railway (II&M) was organized December 11, 1902, to run from Milwaukee to Rockford and then around Chicago to Gary. It built seventy-eight miles from its Rockford base to Aurora and obtained trackage rights over EJ&E to Joliet. In 1904–1905, II&M laid another nineteen miles of track to Delmar, Illinois, where it stopped. The struggling property was reorganized as the Chicago, Milwaukee & Gary in 1908.

In 1897, John R. Walsh, a Chicago banker, bought the bankrupt, flood-damaged 64-mile Evansville & Richmond Railway and renamed it the Southern Indiana Railway. He repaired and extended it to Terre Haute, Indiana, where it delivered coal and limestone shipments to the Chicago & Eastern Illinois. Dissatisfied with his C&EI connection, Walsh incorporated the Chicago Southern Railway in 1906–1907 to build a new 162-mile main line north from

On September 1, 1965, Chicago & Eastern Illinois GP9 236 works northward with a local freight on the Chicago & Western Indiana. It is crossing the Baltimore & Ohio Chicago Terminal diamonds at Oakdale. *Walter E. Zullig*

Terre Haute to Chicago Heights, Illinois, parallel to C&EI's route and the Illinois–Indiana state line. Chicago Southern, which obtained trackage rights over Chicago Terminal Transfer Railroad in 1913, was one of the few Chicago railroads that never carried a revenue passenger. After his banks failed in December 1905, Walsh was arrested for lending depositors' funds to the enterprises he controlled, serving a prison term after his conviction.

Walsh's Indiana and Illinois properties were reorganized in 1910 as the Chicago, Terre Haute & Southeastern Railway. To tap southern Indiana coalfields (for locomotive fuel), the St. Paul leased this line for 999 years on July 1, 1921, and in January 1922 acquired the Chicago, Milwaukee & Gary to link its

Chicago–Omaha main line (former Chicago & Pacific) with the Southeastern at Delmar. The railroad also used Indiana Harbor Belt to reach the Southeastern from Bensenville Yard. After a 1925 bankruptcy, the St. Paul was reorganized in 1928 as the Chicago, Milwaukee, St. Paul & Pacific Railroad, better known as the Milwaukee Road.

The Chicago, Indiana & Southern (CI&S) was a New York Central System project to link the bituminous fields of southern Indiana and Illinois (served by the Big Four) with steel mills in the Chicago area. In 1905–1906, NYC funded construction between Indiana Harbor (East Chicago), Indiana, and Danville, Illinois, chartering CI&S to operate both this line and its Indiana, Illinois & Iowa Railroad (running

In January 1965, Milwaukee Road CFA16-4 number 25C slams the diamonds at Rondout, Illinois, as an Elgin, Joliet & Eastern train waits short of Rockland Road for the train to pass. The tell-tale overhead warnings in the background and bridge abutments were for North Shore's Mundelein branch, which had been abandoned two years earlier. Milwaukee Road was one of only a handful of railroads in the United States to purchase Fairbanks-Morse C-Liners. *Terry Norton*

A single-car eastbound South Shore train rockets over the Baltimore & Ohio main line at Miller (Gary), Indiana, on April 3, 1977. Below, Chesapeake & Ohio U25B 8118 in Chessie system paint leads a blue GP40. Miller was an important interchange between the South Shore and Chessie during the years of C&O ownership (1967–1984). The interchange track is visible above the U-boat. *Don Ellison*

from South Bend, Indiana, to connections in central Illinois).

On July 2, 1910, the Chesapeake & Ohio system bought the last trunk line built to the city. The Chicago, Cincinnati & Louisville Railroad (CC&L) was constructed between Cincinnati and Hammond (HY Tower) via Richmond, Marion, and Peru, Indiana, between 1904 and 1907. From Hammond northwest CC&L used the Hammond Belt Railway (built 1906–1907) to reach Louisville Junction with IHB near 146th and Marquette in Calumet City, Illinois, then on to a connection with IC at Riverdale. Running parallel to well-established Big Four and Pennsylvania routes across Indiana, CC&L was unable to compete. C&O took control when CC&L defaulted on its loans, reorganizing the company as the

Chesapeake & Ohio Railway of Indiana. C&O opted out of the Hammond Belt connection (abandoned about 1926), instead using a paired-track agreement established with Chicago & Erie to the state line and west of there on Chicago & Western Indiana to Chicago. Despite C&O's dominant position as an Eastern bituminous coal hauler, its Chicago connection never became one of its major routes. From 1911 through 1917 C&O offered through passenger service from Dearborn Station to points east of Cincinnati, after that reverting to its prior practice of through-routing feature trains with the much faster Big Four. In 1925 C&O moved its remaining local passenger train to IC's Central Station, but cut that service back to Hammond on June 30, 1933.

RISE OF A RAILROAD CAPITAL, 1848-1910

AT&SF	Atchison, Topeka & Santa Fe	**C&RI**	Chicago & Rock Island	**EC**	East Chicago (PRR)
B&O	Baltimore & Ohio	**C&WI**	Chicago & Western Indiana	**EJ&E**	Elgin, Joliet & Eastern
B&OCT	Baltimore & Ohio Chicago Terminal	**CB&Q**	Chicago, Burlington & Quincy	**G&CU**	Galena & Chicago Union (C&NW)
BRC	Belt Railway of Chicago	**CC&L**	Chicago, Cincinnati & Louisville (C&O)	**GT**	Grand Trunk
C&A	Chicago & Alton	**CD&V**	Chicago, Danville & Vincennes (C&EI)	**IC**	Illinois Central
C&ATL	Chicago & Atlantic (Erie)	**CGW**	Chicago Great Western	**IHB**	Indiana Harbor Belt
C&CT	Chicago & Calumet Terminal (B&OCT)	**CH&W**	Chicago, Hammond & Western (IHB)	**IN**	Illinois Northern (ATSF)
C&EI	Chicago & Eastern Illinois	**CI&L**	Chicago, Indianapolis & Louisville (Monon)	**IW**	Illinois Western (C&NW)
C&GW	Chicago & Great Western (WC)	**CJ**	Chicago Junction (NYC)	**J&C**	Joliet & Chicago (C&A)
C&IW	Chicago & Illinois Western (IC)	**CLS&E**	Chicago, Lake Shore & Eastern (EJ&E)	**LNA&C**	Louisville, New Albany & Chicago (CI&L)
C&M	Chicago & Milwaukee (C&NW)	**CM&N**	Chicago, Madison & Northern (IC)	**LS&MS**	Lake Shore & Michigan Southern (NYC)
C&NP	Chicago & Northern Pacific (WC)	**CT**	Chicago Terminal & Transfer (B&OCT)	**MC**	Michigan Central
C&NW	Chicago & North Western	**CUTC**	Chicago Union Transfer (BRC)	**MILW**	Chicago, Milwaukee & St. Paul

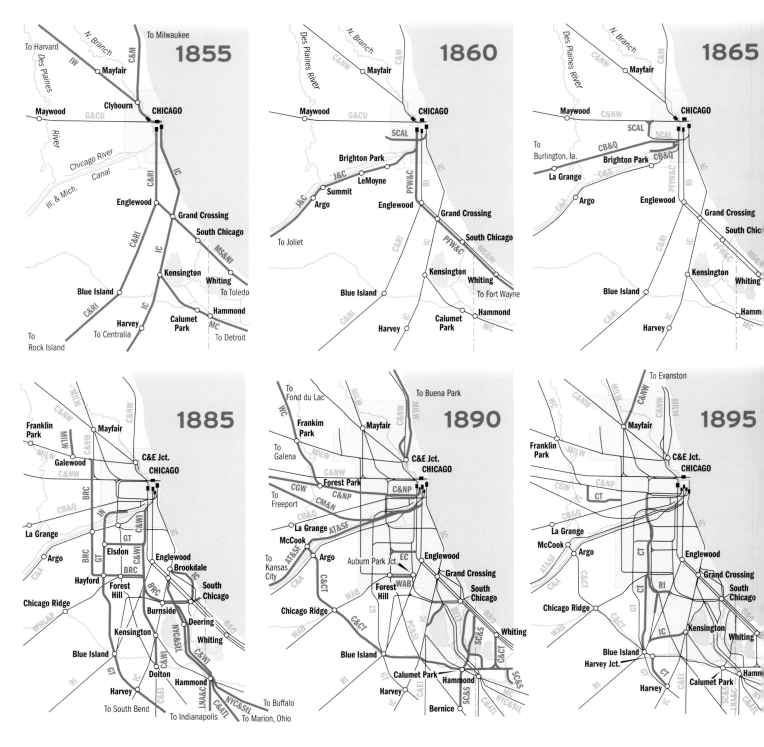

MS&NI	Michigan Southern & Northern Indiana (LS&MS)
NYC&StL	New York, Chicago & St. Louis (Nickel Plate)
PCC&StL	Pittsburgh, Cincinnati, Chicago & St. Louis (PRR)
PFW&C	Pittsburgh, Fort Wayne & Chicago (PRR)
RI	Chicago, Rock Island & Pacific
SCAL	St. Charles Air Line
SC&S	South Chicago & Southern (PRR)
SOO	Minneapolis, St. Paul & Sault Ste. Marie
TR	Terminal Railroad (IHB)
USY&T	Union Stock Yards & Transit (CJ)
WAB	Wabash
WC	Wisconsin Central
WStL&P	Wabash, St. Louis & Pacific (WAB)

Industrial Railways and Short Lines

The Chicago & Illinois Western Railroad (owned and operated by IC, but using its own equipment) was constructed in 1906–1907 and ran parallel to IC's Iowa Division from a connection with the Panhandle near Western Avenue to Hawthorne, then 13.59 miles farther west toward a junction with C&CT (later B&OCT) and IHB at McCook. Nearby, at Western Electric's Hawthorne Works in Cicero, the Manufacturers Junction Railway (MJ) was built in 1906 to switch incoming materials and outbound carloads of telephone equipment for Ma Bell. Chicago, West Pullman & Southern Railway (later Railroad) was a fourteen-mile line built in the 1880s to serve Wisconsin Steel's South Chicago mill. The aptly named Chicago Short Line owned less than a mile of track (plus eleven miles of trackage rights on Rock Island, B&O, and other roads) and served the Iroquois Iron Company (later Youngstown Sheet & Tube) in East Chicago, Indiana.

Manufacturers Junction Railway EMD SW1 number 23 hauls a cut of cars near Cermak Road in Cicero on May 1, 2009. MJ was formed to serve the sprawling Western Electric Hawthorne Works factory. The plant closed in 1983, but the railroad survived to serve other customers on its trackage. The railroad subsequently ceased operations and in 2012 its classic SW1 locomotives were cut up. *Ray Weart*

Eastern Railroad Lake Terminals

Large Eastern railroads, including the Philadelphia & Reading; the Lehigh Valley; and the Delaware, Lackawanna & Western, operated terminals along the Chicago River to handle coal and other bulk commodities transported by boat across the Great Lakes. Between 1913 and 1936, the Erie Railroad's marine fleet ferried cars from its 18th Street freight yard to three river terminals on the North Side. The Lake Michigan Car Ferry Transportation Company served as the Chicago extension of the Wisconsin & Michigan Railway by operating tugboats and barges carrying railroad cars between Peshtigo Harbor, Michigan, and South Chicago, where the Rock Island switched the fleet. This service began on August 29, 1895, but was unsuccessful. The boats stopped running after the 1909 season, and W&M abandoned its line in 1938.

Track Elevation, the Lakefront Ordinance, and IC Electrification

Chicago's population zoomed past the one million mark in the late 1880s. The city's heavy rail traffic—roughly 1,300 trains per day—became a vexing dilemma as it blocked streets with ever greater frequency. Even worse, trains killed three hundred to four hundred Chicagoans annually as they tried to cross the tracks.

Successful elevation of the IC for the World's Columbian Exposition induced City Hall to encourage the other railroads to elevate their trunk lines through densely populated areas. A series of ordinances was negotiated, the first of which, enacted July 9, 1894, required elevation of the Rock Island–Lake Shore & Michigan Southern main line between Archer Avenue and 69th Street. Track elevation took more than twenty years to complete, but it improved traffic flow and dramatically cut the number of railroad-pedestrian fatalities.

An enormous improvement program was executed by Chicago & North Western in the early twentieth century coincident with construction of its new North Western Station

Illinois Central electrified its commuter service in 1926 with a fleet of 280 cars (half and half powered cars and trailers) to work a schedule of 542 weekday trains that carried an estimated 121,000 passengers. IC's suburban service was in transition when George W. Kowanski made this image of its 1920s-era all-steel electrics passing brand-new Highliners in September 1971. Like their predecessors, the Highliners would serve for more than four decades before being replaced in the 2010s. *George W. Kowanski*

at Madison and Canal Streets. (See Chapter 2.) Included in this extensive reconfiguration of C&NW's Chicago terminals was the New Line between Mayfair and St. Francis, Wisconsin, built parallel to the original Chicago–Milwaukee main line between 1903 and 1906, and construction of the Des Plaines Valley Railroad between 1911 and 1912, linking the New Line with Proviso Yard via Des Plaines.

Smoke abatement was another long-standing public concern in Chicago. A massive study in 1915 proposed electrifying 3,439 track-miles in the city and its suburbs to eliminate locomotive smoke. Although this extensive wiring of Chicago's railways was never carried out, the Lakefront Ordinance, passed by the city council in 1919, required the electrification of Illinois Central's suburban passenger service by 1927. (See Chapter 2.) It was expected that IC's freight and through passenger service would be electrified at a later date, but dieselization made that unnecessary.

Insull Interurbans

Interurban railways adapted electric streetcar technology for suburban and intercity transportation. From modest beginnings in the 1890s, the American interurban network boomed between 1900 and 1910, constructing some 10,000 miles of new electrified rail lines that successfully competed with established steam railroads by offering more frequent service at lower prices. Yet these new lines were doomed by the advent of the automobile. From peak mileage of 15,580 in 1916, the interurban network shriveled to next to nothing over the following four decades.

Foremost among the fanciful interurban projects that were never consummated was the Chicago–New York Electric Air Line Railroad, which proposed a 742-mile double-track route between its namesake cities without a single curve (despite the multitude of rivers, lakes, and mountains in its path).

Under control of Samuel Insull, North Shore commenced direct downtown service via the L. On August 6, 1919, North Shore began serving its new terminal on the Loop at Adams and Wabash Streets; three years later it began operating trains to 63rd and Dorchester on the South Side. In 1962, Richard Solomon checked in at Chicago's YMCA and requested a room overlooking the L so that he could take photos of the North Shore. "The desk clerk must have thought I was crazy," he recalled. *Richard Jay Solomon*

The cost of building this 90-mile-per-hour speedway proved insurmountable; just fifteen miles of the line were completed near Gary before the company folded.

Chicago's three best-known interurban lines were famously upgraded under the ownership and management of Samuel Insull, who also headed Commonwealth Edison and the L system. The Waukegan & North Shore Rapid Transit Company was formed October 1891. Later renamed the Chicago & Milwaukee Electric Railway, it grew into a seventy-three-mile Evanston–Milwaukee interurban (with a branch to Mundelein). Bankruptcy in 1908 allowed Insull to take over, and on May 1, 1916, he reorganized

the company as the Chicago, North Shore & Milwaukee Railroad (CNS&M), known universally as the North Shore. By virtue of his control of the L system, Insull extended the interurban line directly to downtown Chicago in 1919. Insull's most significant North Shore improvement was the twenty-four-mile double-track Skokie Valley Route from Howard Street (near Chicago's northern limits) to North Chicago Junction, which opened June 5, 1926, bypassing slow street-running on the lakefront while making North Shore's Chicago–Milwaukee service the fastest in the interurban industry.

Having invested in Indiana utilities, Insull expanded his holdings on June 29,

1925, with the purchase of the Chicago, Lake Shore & South Bend, a line running from South Bend, Indiana, to an Illinois Central connection at Kensington (using IC-owned Kensington & Eastern Railroad between there and the state line). He renamed it Chicago South Shore & South Bend Railroad (CSS&SB), commonly known as the South Shore. In addition to rebuilding the line and replacing its wooden cars with modern steel ones, Insull's management changed South Shore's electrification from alternating to direct current to make it compatible with the new IC installation. Through electric service to downtown Chicago via IC began August 29, 1926.

Insull's third major interurban acquisition was the Chicago, Aurora & Elgin Railroad (CA&E), which extended from a connection with the L at Laramie Street in Chicago to Aurora, Batavia, Geneva, and Elgin on the Fox River, some thirty-five miles west. The distinction of the Roarin' Elgin was that it largely used an electrified third rail to distribute power to trains, rather than overhead catenary.

Above: This view of a stationary North Shore interurban train was exposed from a CTA train at the Wabash Portal on July 20, 1958. The North Shore train was stored on the L between runs. *Richard Jay Solomon*; **Below:** In April 1962, a one-car locomotive-hauled North Shore special has just swung off the main line and onto the Mundelein Branch headed westbound in Lake Bluff. The train has crossed Scranton Avenue and is most likely headed towards the Skokie Valley line that diverged from the Libertyville Branch just ahead. *Terry Norton*

Above: South Shore's Little Joe electric 802 works a freight in March 1981. Originally built by GE for the Soviet Union, the double-end electrics could not be shipped owing to Cold War tensions in the late 1940s. South Shore bought three of the orphaned electrics, nicknamed Little Joes in reference to Soviet General Secretary of the Central Committee of the Communist Party, Joseph Stalin. The railroad acquired 10 GP38-2s in January 1981, and phased out use of the Little Joes over the next two years. *Mike Abalos;* **Below:** Chicago, Aurora & Elgin was an interurban electric line that connected its namesake western suburbs with a downtown terminal on the L at Wells Street, pictured on August 12, 1939. The electric line was famous for its extensive third-rail power distribution. CA&E ended regularly scheduled passenger operations in July 1957, and it was abandoned in 1959 despite proposals to revive the line. *J. Michael Gruber collection*

Insull interests assumed control on March 10, 1926, and continued investing in the property, including starting a planned bypass similar to North Shore's Skokie Valley Route. CA&E completed a mile of track from its main line at Bellwood southward to the new town site of Westchester on October 1, 1926, with plans to extend a high-speed line west to Aurora through farmlands and a hamlet called Utopia. The Depression, though, killed the bypass, and the orphaned Westchester branch was abandoned in 1951.

Insull lost control of his interurbans during the Depression, yet these railways survived the 1930s intact and profited from the crush of riders during World War II. CA&E operated with few changes until September 20, 1953, when the railroad's CTA connection was cut due to construction of the new CTA line in the Congress Expressway median. Afterwards CA&E terminated at Forest Park, necessitating an inconvenient train change to reach Chicago. Most of the Roarin' Elgin's riders defected to North Western's commuter service or the highways thereafter. Approval to discontinue passenger service was granted on July 3, 1957, and CA&E infamously shut down service midday, stranding its remaining commuters downtown. Following abandonment of freight operations in 1959, CA&E's right-of-way became the Illinois Prairie Path—one of the earliest rails-to-trails conversions.

North Shore suffered long strikes in 1938 and 1948 while postwar construction of the Edens and Northwest (later Kennedy) Expressways reduced patronage. Its original route through the lakefront suburbs was abandoned in 1955, and authority to shut down the entire system was exercised on January 21, 1963. CTA took over the southernmost five miles of the Skokie Valley Route on April 20, 1964, operating shuttles to Howard Street as the Skokie Swift, while C&NW bought portions of the railroad north of Skokie because CNS&M's track was in better shape than its parallel line through the Skokie Valley.

Only the South Shore, with its fast route to downtown Chicago and profitable freight traffic in heavily industrialized northwest Indiana, survives. In 1954–1956 the railroad built a grade-separated bypass from Hammond to Gary alongside the new Indiana Toll Road, speeding service. Chesapeake & Ohio bought CSS&SB on January 3, 1967, and continued investing as new coal-burning power plants came on-line. The Northern Indiana Commuter Transportation District was formed in 1977 to foreclose abandonment of the by-then unprofitable passenger service. New equipment to replace the Insull-era passenger cars began arriving in 1982. NICTD began operating the passenger service directly in 1989, with holding company Anacostia & Pacific acquiring the freight operations that continue today.

Coming off the IC-owned, South Shore–leased Kensington & Eastern (K&E) in November 1978, an eight-car CSS&SB passenger train crosses the Illinois Central Gulf freight and through passenger tracks at Kensington to reach ICG's electric lines and the Kensington platform. South Shore ridership boomed in 1926 after its trains began operating through Kensington to downtown Chicago over the IC. A second connection from the K&E to the now–Metra Electric lines was put in service in 2012 to expedite the 110 or so daily passenger movements through the Kensington interlocking. Canadian National contributes about twenty daily freight movements. *Don Ellison*

Amtrak and Metra

After World War II, rail passenger travel declined rapidly, and Chicago's terminals became ghost towns. Notwithstanding the increasingly empty intercity trains, public sentiment favored preservation of core rail passenger services, which led to the federal government's creation of the National Railroad Passenger Corporation, known as Amtrak. On April 30, 1971, railroads that elected to "join" Amtrak (by contributing to its capital) discontinued their passenger trains, with Amtrak subsidizing the operation of a basic nationwide network starting the next day. In a few short months, Amtrak consolidated its Chicago operations at Union Station, thus accomplishing a unified Chicago long-distance passenger terminal, which decades of civic effort and planning had failed to achieve.

Instead of abandoning unprofitable suburban services, Chicago's commuter railroads encouraged the Illinois General Assembly to form the Regional Transportation Authority (RTA) in 1974, which used a dedicated sales tax increment to cover the deficits of trains and buses within its six-county territory. Railroads initially continued to operate the commuter trains over their own lines with their own employees. However, the bankruptcy and reorganization of the Rock Island and Milwaukee Road threatened service on those important lines. The RTA organized the Northeast Illinois Regional Commuter Railroad Corporation (NIRCRC) to acquire these properties from the bankrupt railroads' estates in the early 1980s, hiring its own crews to operate them. Financial difficulties led the state to reorganize the RTA in 1983, creating three service boards to operate the CTA, suburban buses (Pace), and the commuter trains. Rail services were rebranded as Metra in 1984, covering both the lines operated directly

A pair of Metra F40PHM-2s, a model unique to the Chicago-area commuter railroad, lead an outbound BNSF train at Roosevelt Road on June 22, 2004. The passenger trains of BNSF and its Burlington-side predecessors have terminated at Union Station since 1882. *Brian Solomon*

by NIRCRC and the C&NW and Burlington Northern lines, which those railroads operated under purchase of service agreements. Metra acquired the IC electric operation in 1987, taking over the former Alton service to Joliet at the same time, and in 1993 Metra assumed control of the former Wabash service as well, extending it from Orland Park to Manhattan in 2006.

Top Left: An eastbound South Shore train led by modernized Insull-era car 28 rolls past a westbound freight behind Little Joe electric 803 in September 1977. South Shore lengthened thirty-six of its 1920s-vintage sixty-foot cars to seventy-eight feet during the 1940s, adding air conditioning and wide picture windows to later rebuilds such as 28. The 803 has been preserved at the Illinois Railway Museum; sister 802 is at the Lake Shore Railway Museum in North East, Pennsylvania, near its Erie birthplace. *Don Ellison;*
Top Right: Although Amtrak consolidated most of its Chicago long-distance services at Union Station in 1971, its *James Whitcomb Riley/George Washington* (Chicago–Washington D.C and Newport News) and Illinois Central services continued to use IC's Central Station through March 5, 1972. This was a carryover from New York Central days, when Big Four trains called at Central rather than LaSalle Street Station because they operated over IC north of Kankakee. This view of the eastbound *James Whitcomb Riley* before departure from Central Station was made in September 1971. *George W. Kowanski;* **Right:** Amtrak focused its operations on Union Station, thus allowing this station to function as a unified long-distance hub. On August 28, 1996, a former GO Transit GP40TC departs Union Station with train 347, the Illinois Zephyr. This utilitarian consist was a far cry from the sleek Zephyrs of the 1930s. *Brian Solomon*

Above: On February 21, 2003, an outbound Metra train from LaSalle Street Station on the Rock Island District approaches 16th Street Tower. The Regional Transportation Authority was established in 1973 to fund unprofitable commuter services in the six-county Chicago area. It rescued Rock Island's service after that line descended into bankruptcy in 1975 and ceased operating in 1980. Chicago suburban services were rebranded as Metra (short for Metropolitan Rail) in 1984. *Brian Solomon;*
Below: After Amtrak assumed operation of most intercity passenger services, Norfolk & Western continued to operate a single weekday suburban train on its former Wabash line to Orland Park. This lonely train slows for its Orland Park station stop on May 25, 1979. Chicago's Regional Transportation Authority began subsidizing N&W's commuter operation in 1978. Today, the old Wabash route hosts Metra's SouthWest Service, which has been extended beyond Orland Park to Manhattan and now features fifteen trains each way on weekdays. *Mike Abalos*

Today's Chicago Railroads

Compared to the frenzied construction period up until 1910, relatively few changes occurred in Chicago's trunk line network in the period between passage of the Transportation Act of 1920 (the high water mark of federal regulation of the industry) and the 1960s. Control of the Alton passed to Baltimore & Ohio in 1931, and in 1947 the Alton was sold to the Gulf, Mobile & Ohio, extending that system to Chicago. Also in 1947 the Pere Marquette was acquired by Chesapeake & Ohio, resulting in C&O moving its freight operations into PM's leased Rockwell Street Yard.

The 1960s, though, saw rapid change as the industry responded to inflation and truck competition. In 1964 Norfolk & Western reached Chicago as result of its merger with Nickel Plate Road and leasing of Wabash. Until it merged with Southern in 1982, N&W made few changes to its Chicago lines, but since then Norfolk Southern has abandoned most of the former Wabash Pumpkin Vine east to Ohio, while cutting Wabash's original Chicago line between Manhattan and Risk, Illinois, in favor of IC haulage rights.

Missouri Pacific began buying Chicago & Eastern Illinois stock in the early 1960s and won regulatory approval to control that company in 1967. But the Interstate Commerce Commission imposed conditions, including the sale of C&EI's Evansville, Indiana main line to Louisville & Nashville (implemented June 6, 1969). MP and L&N shared ownership of the C&EI from Chicago to Woodland Junction, Illinois. In 1971 L&N bought the Monon, giving it a second Chicago line.

This photograph of Hohman Avenue Tower in Hammond, Indiana was taken on November 5, 2006. The tower was closed in 2001, but wasn't demolished for another decade. The end came on May 10, 2011. *Scott Muskopf*

Above Left: In December 1984, Norfolk & Western SD35 1568 leads Norfolk Southern train CD-1 (Chicago to Decatur, Illinois) through Oak Lawn. NS operated the former Wabash as a through route until 1990, when it obtained trackage rights on Illinois Central from Chicago to Gibson City, Illinois. At that time it abandoned its line beyond Manhattan to Risk. Now primarily the route of Metra's SouthWest Service, NS still owns and dispatches the Manhattan line, which hosts a nocturnal local freight as well as a four-day per week *RoadRailer* between Chicago Ridge and Belt Junction (to/from a connection with Union Pacific). *Mike Abalos;* **Above Right:** In October 1966, about two years after Norfolk & Western leased Wabash, Craig Willett photographed the St. Louis-bound *Banner Blue* running on Chicago & Western Indiana and crossing the Pennsylvania Railroad at 21st Street. The equipment reflects the Nickel Plate & Wabash merger: former NKP GP9s, an original N&W baggage car, and two former NKP coaches lead the Wabash-heritage heavyweight diner and parlor-observation. *Craig Willett;* **Below:** Louisville & Nashville's *Danville Flyer* rolls past on April 24, 1971. L&N was among the eighteen railroads that joined Amtrak on May 1, 1971. The former C&EI route was not included in Amtrak's system, and the line has been freight-only since except for periodic detours of the *Texas Eagle. John Gruber*

New York Central and Pennsylvania merged to form Penn Central (PC) on February 1, 1968. This prompted substantial changes in Chicago's railroad map. A post-merger connection between PRR and NYC lines at Hammond permitted the abandonment of the NYC through South Chicago and the shifting of the former NYC passenger trains into Union Station after October 26, 1968. PC later abandoned most of the former Michigan Central's Joliet branch.

PC's financial collapse on June 21, 1970 spurred Congress to combine PC with other bankrupt Eastern carriers, including Erie (by then Erie Lackawanna), as the Consolidated Rail Corporation, or Conrail, which began operations on April 1, 1976. This began a widespread rationalization and consolidation of the northeastern railroad system that included abandonment of EL's Chicago main line and most of the former PRR Panhandle line.

Chicago & North Western merged with Chicago Great Western in 1968, which resulted in gradual abandonment of CGW's line through the western suburbs. In 1970, Burlington merged with its corporate parents, Great Northern and Northern Pacific, to form Burlington Northern. Two years later, Illinois Central and Gulf, Mobile & Ohio merged as Illinois Central Gulf. Neither consolidation

A westbound Erie Lackawanna intermodal train approaches the complicated crossing in Griffith, Indiana, in March 1976, guarded by the interlocking tower to the left. At Griffith, EL crossed Grand Trunk Western, New York Central's Joliet branch, and Elgin, Joliet & Eastern; Chesapeake & Ohio of Indiana entered the EL main line here westbound. Just days remained before EL would lose its heavy freight traffic as a result of Conrail. Today EL and NYC are abandoned, Canadian National has transformed the area with new connections between its EJ&E and GTW lines, and the tower has been closed and moved north to a museum that also includes GTW's former Griffith station and preserved EJ&E equipment. *Don Ellison*

caused substantial changes in Chicago, but in the 1980s ICG sold its secondary lines. The Iowa Division became the Chicago Central & Pacific (CC&P) in 1985, and former Alton routes (south of Joliet) were sold to Chicago, Missouri & Western in 1987. These changes were short lived. CM&W failed a couple years after it began operations, which allowed the Southern Pacific system, through a subsidiary, to buy the former Alton route between East St. Louis and Joliet (with rights to Chicago) in November 1989. ICG (by then renamed Illinois Central) reacquired CC&P in 1996.

Above: At Ingalton (West Chicago), Chicago Great Western maintained a small yard for interchange with Elgin, Joliet & Eastern. CGW generally ran two road freight trains a day in each direction, plus a local powered by its two GP7s. *Terry Norton;*
Below: A pair of former CB&Q GP9s leading a recently painted Cascade green wooden caboose pass Canal and 18th Streets shortly after the BN merger. Although merger of Burlington, Great Northern, Northern Pacific, and Spokane, Portland & Seattle created America's largest railroad, initially operations in Chicago stayed mostly the same. *George W. Kowanski*

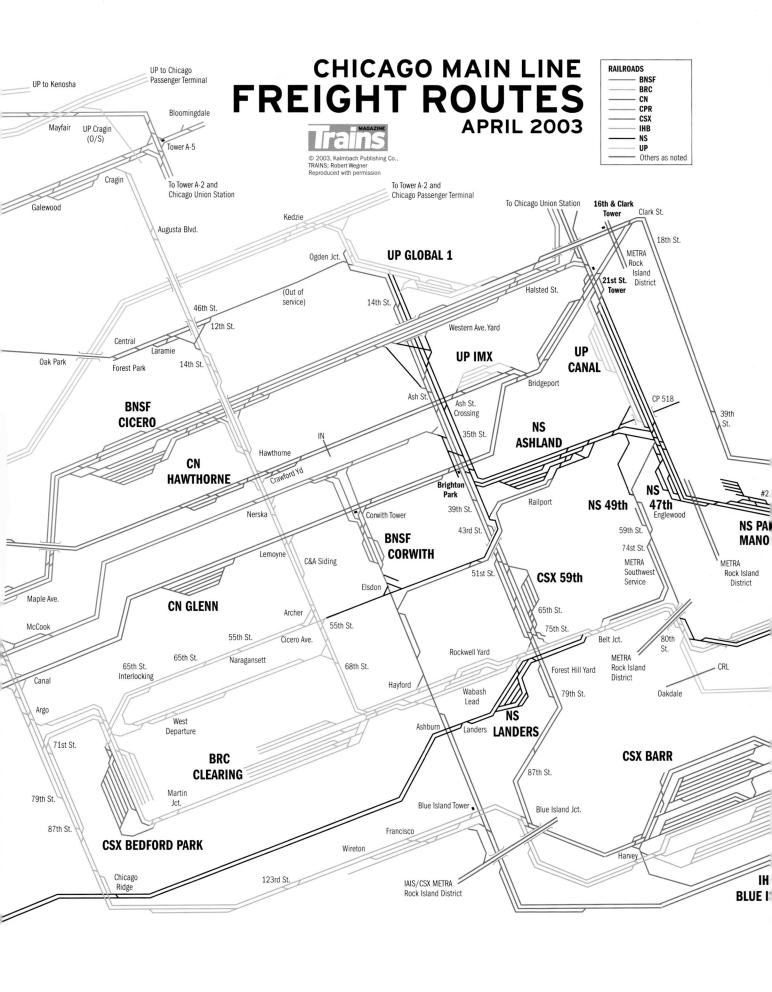

CHICAGO MAIN LINE
FREIGHT ROUTES
APRIL 2003

Trains MAGAZINE

© 2003, Kalmbach Publishing Co.,
TRAINS; Robert Wegner
Reproduced with permission

RAILROADS

	BNSF
	BRC
	CN
	CPR
	CSX
	IHB
	NS
	UP
	Others as noted

UP to Kenosha

UP to Chicago
Passenger Terminal

Bloomingdale

Mayfair

UP Cragin
(O/S)

Tower A-5

Cragin

To Tower A-2 and
Chicago Union Station

Galewood

To Tower A-2 and
Chicago Passenger Terminal

To Chicago Union Station

16th & Clark
Tower

Clark St.

18th St.

Augusta Blvd.

Kedzie

METRA
Rock
Island
District

Ogden Jct.

UP GLOBAL 1

21st St.
Tower

(Out of
service)

14th St.

Halsted St.

46th St.

12th St.

Western Ave. Yard

UP IMX

**UP
CANAL**

Central

Laramie

CP 518

39th
St.

Oak Park

14th St.

Ash St.

Bridgeport

Forest Park

Ash St.
Crossing

**NS
ASHLAND**

**BNSF
CICERO**

35th St.

IN

Hawthorne

**NS
47th**

NS 49th

**CN
HAWTHORNE**

Crawford Yd.

Brighton
Park

Railport

Englewood

**NS PA
MANO**

#2

Nerska

Corwith Tower

39th St.

59th St.

43rd St.

74st St.

METRA
Rock Island
District

Lemoyne

C&A Siding

**BNSF
CORWITH**

METRA
Southwest
Service

Maple Ave.

Elsdon

51st St.

CSX 59th

McCook

CN GLENN

Archer

55th St.

65th St.

75th St.

Belt Jct.

80th
St.

55th St.

Cicero Ave.

CRL

65th St.
Interlocking

65th St.

Naragansett

68th St.

Rockwell Yard

METRA
Rock Island
District

Canal

Hayford

Forest Hill Yard

Oakdale

Argo

West
Departure

Wabash
Lead

79th St.

71st St.

Ashburn

Landers

**NS
LANDERS**

79th St.

**BRC
CLEARING**

CSX BARR

Martin
Jct.

87th St.

87th St.

Blue Island Tower

Blue Island Jct.

CSX BEDFORD PARK

Francisco

Chicago
Ridge

123rd St.

Wireton

Harvey

IAIS/CSX METRA
Rock Island District

**IH
BLUE I**

LAKE MICHIGAN

Grand Central Station
Union Station
C&NW Passenger Termial

CSS&SB, IC Randolph St. Station

Randolph St.
Van Buren St.

Dearborn Station
Central Station

State St.

La Salle St. Station

16th St.
22nd St.
26th St.
31st St.
Douglas

16th St.

Oakland
43rd St.
CSS&SB
Kenwood
Hyde Park

IC

57th St.
60th St.
Woodlawn
67th St.
Stony Island Ave.
Bryn Mawr
South Shore
Windsor Park
Cheltenham
81st St.
87st St.
90st St.
91st St.

EJ&E

76th St.
81st St.

Stony Is. Ave.

Brookdale

IC
B&O
NYC
PRR

C&O, CCC&StL, MC

North Ave.

C&NW
PRR MILW

Halsted St.

31st St.

21st St.

NYC

NYC&StL

CRI&P PRR

Brookdale
Essex

Grand
Crossing

NYC&StL

C&O

NYC&StL

Burns

Western Ave.

PRR

Robey St.

Western Ave.

Halsted
St.

C&WI, CI&L, ERIE,
C&EI, GTW, WAB

Bridgeport

CHICAGO
JUNCTION

Halsted St.
Racine Ave.

Ashland Ave.

GTW

55th St.
Englewood
Normal Park
Hamilton Park
Auburn Park
81st St.
83rd St.
Hammond Jct.

BRC
WAB

58th St.

Englewood
Normal Park
Hamilton Park

Euclid Park

C&WI
C&EI

C&NW

CB&Q

PM

55th St.

59th St.

PRR

Gresham
Gresham Jct.

Kedzie Ave.

Western
Ave.

Ash
St.

C&A

Chandler

Dewey

Brainerd

95th St.
99th St.

PM

CRI

Homan Ave.

CR&I
NI
PM

Brighton Park

Western
Ave.

PRR

B&OCT

63rd St.
PM

Marlboro

Forest Hill

B&O Jct.

Beverly
Hills

Beverly
Jct.
Longwood

Walden

Tracy

Kedzie
Ave.

Lawndale Ave.

Corwith
CR&I

IN

Morrel Park

Elsdon

Glendale
59th St.
Chicago
Lawn

Marquette
Park

BRC

Landers

B&OCT

Tracy

Crawford
Ave.

Corwith
Jct.

Nerska
Le Moyne

GTW

Evergreen
Park

Tracy Ave.

BRC

48th Ave.

Cicero

Hyman
Ave.
Hawthorne Ave.

Hayford

Ashburn

Evergreen Park

Ste. Maria

Mt. Green

AUSTIN

Morton
Park

BRC

WABASH

Austin Ave.

Central Ave.

Clyde

Ogden Ave.

Glenn

Oak Lawn

SOO
CGW
B&OCT
B&OCT

Ridgeland

Berwyn

Berwyn

OAK PARK

IC

Harlem Ave.

Lathrop
Ave.

Parkway

BRC

River
Forest

Forest Park

RIVER

Riverside

Riverside

C&IW

IHB

Chicago Ridge

WESTERN
CENTRAL

MAYWOOD

Tuxedo
Park

Summit

TERMINAL
IHB

Broadview

Worth

Bellewood

Brookfield

McCook

McCook

Argo

CHICAGO & ALTON

ILLINOIS

BALTIMORE & OHIO
INDIANA HARBOR BELT

Congress Park

Gary

Hodgkins

Drainage
Canal

B&O

Oakridge

La Grange (Fifth Ave.)

La Grange (Stone Ave.)

CHICAGO, BURLINGTON & QUINCY

CHICAGO

ATCHISON, TOPEKA & SANTA FE

CHICAGO & ILLINOIS WESTERN

Mt. Forest

Calumet

Hillside

Western Springs

Willow Springs

Willow Springs

Ogden
Ditch

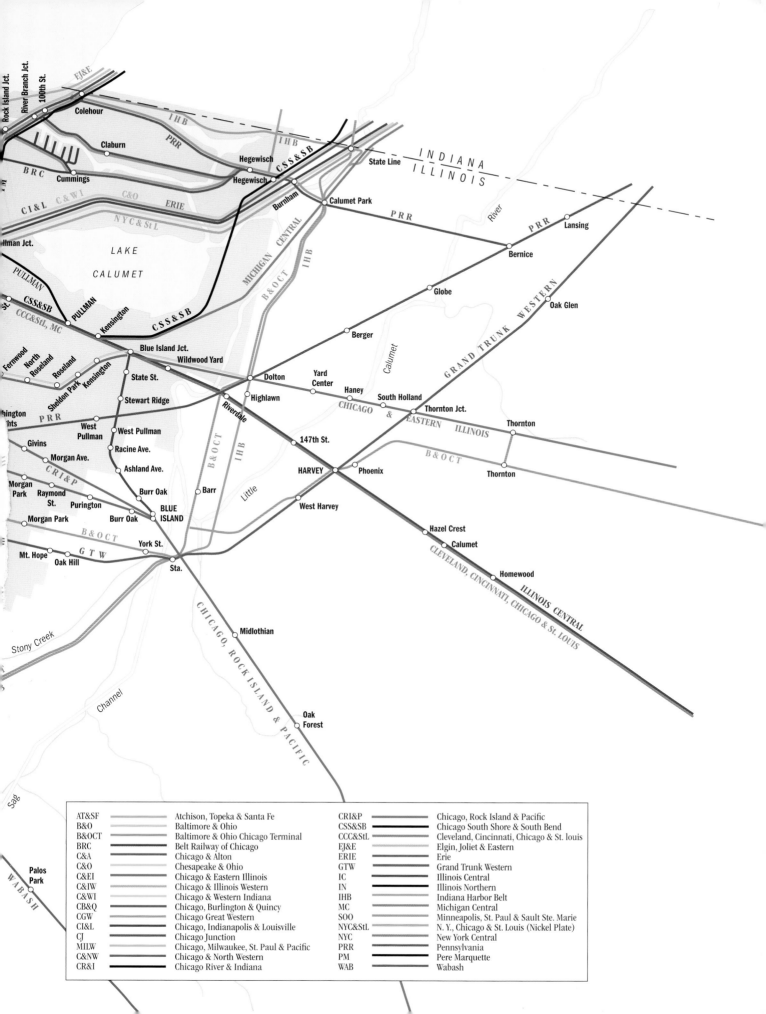

Rock Island Jct.
River Branch Jct.
100th St.
EJ&E
Colehour
IHB
IHB
Claburn
PRR
BRC
Cummings
Hegewisch
CSS&SB
Hegewisch
State Line
INDIANA
ILLINOIS
Burnham
Calumet Park
PRR
River
PRR
Lansing
CI&L
C&WI
C&O
ERIE
NYC&StL
MICHIGAN CENTRAL
IHB
Bernice
Ilman Jct.
LAKE
CALUMET
Globe
Oak Glen
PULLMAN
B&OCT
GRAND TRUNK WESTERN
CSS&SB
St.
CCC&StL, MC
PULLMAN
Kensington
CSS&SB
Berger
Calumet
Fernwood
North Roseland
Roseland
Blue Island Jct.
Kensington
Wildwood Yard
Dolton
Yard Center
Haney
South Holland
Thornton Jct.
Thornton
State St.
Sheldon Park
Highlawn
CHICAGO
&
EASTERN
ILLINOIS
Stewart Ridge
Riverdale
147th St.
Thornton
hington hts
PRR
West Pullman
B&OCT
B&OCT
Givins
West Pullman
Racine Ave.
HARVEY
Phoenix
Morgan Ave.
Ashland Ave.
Hazel Crest
CRI&P
Calumet
Morgan Park
Raymond St.
Burr Oak
Barr
West Harvey
Purington
Little
Homewood
Morgan Park
Burr Oak
BLUE ISLAND
CLEVELAND, CINCINNATI, CHICAGO & St. LOUIS
ILLINOIS CENTRAL
B&OCT
York St.
Mt. Hope
GTW
Oak Hill
Sta.
Midlothian
CHICAGO, ROCK ISLAND & PACIFIC
Stony Creek
Channel
Oak Forest
Sag
Palos Park
WABASH

AT&SF		Atchison, Topeka & Santa Fe	CRI&P		Chicago, Rock Island & Pacific
B&O		Baltimore & Ohio	CSS&SB		Chicago South Shore & South Bend
B&OCT		Baltimore & Ohio Chicago Terminal	CCC&StL		Cleveland, Cincinnati, Chicago & St. louis
BRC		Belt Railway of Chicago	EJ&E		Elgin, Joliet & Eastern
C&A		Chicago & Alton	ERIE		Erie
C&O		Chesapeake & Ohio	GTW		Grand Trunk Western
C&EI		Chicago & Eastern Illinois	IC		Illinois Central
C&IW		Chicago & Illinois Western	IN		Illinois Northern
C&WI		Chicago & Western Indiana	IHB		Indiana Harbor Belt
CB&Q		Chicago, Burlington & Quincy	MC		Michigan Central
CGW		Chicago Great Western	SOO		Minneapolis, St. Paul & Sault Ste. Marie
CI&L		Chicago, Indianapolis & Louisville	NYC&StL		N.Y., Chicago & St. Louis (Nickel Plate)
CJ		Chicago Junction	NYC		New York Central
MILW		Chicago, Milwaukee, St. Paul & Pacific	PRR		Pennsylvania
C&NW		Chicago & North Western	PM		Pere Marquette
CR&I		Chicago River & Indiana	WAB		Wabash

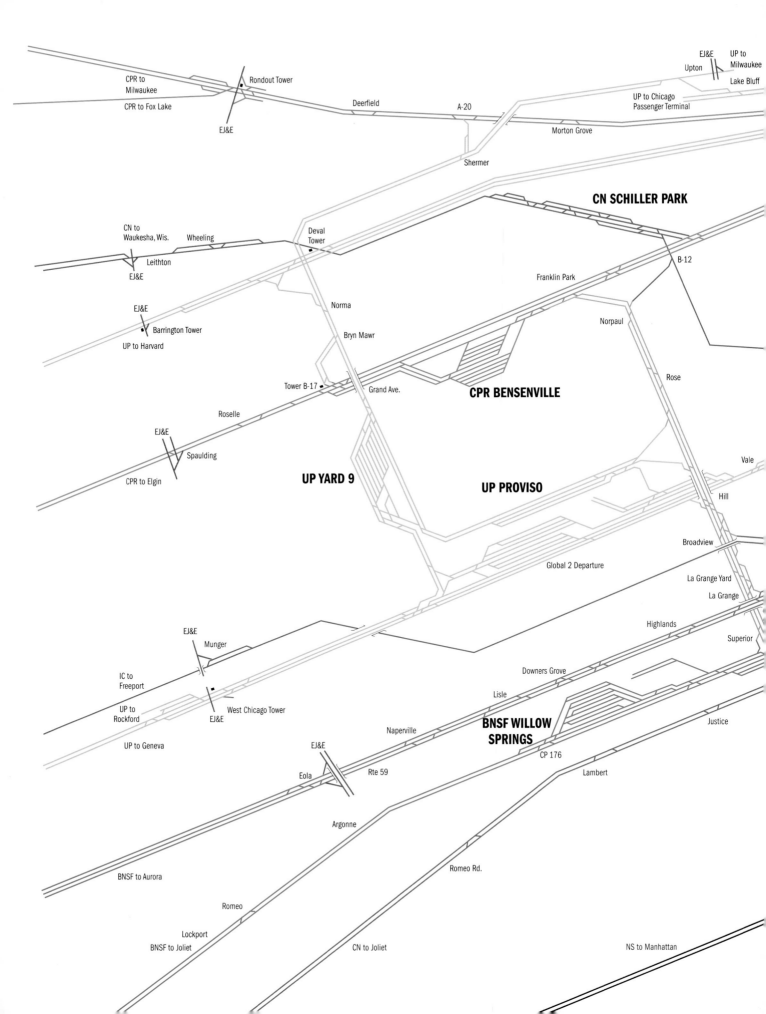

CHICAGO RAILROADS, 1928
HOW THE PASSENGER TRAINS REACHED THE LOOP

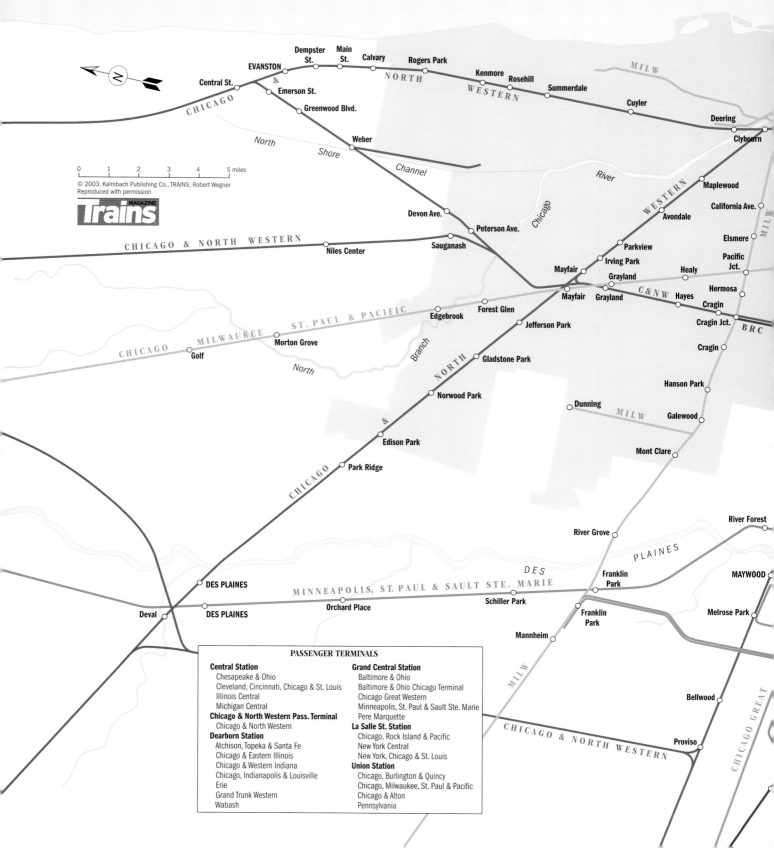

© 2003, Kalmbach Publishing Co., TRAINS; Robert Wegner
Reproduced with permission

Trains MAGAZINE

0 1 2 3 4 5 miles

PASSENGER TERMINALS

Central Station
  Chesapeake & Ohio
  Cleveland, Cincinnati, Chicago & St. Louis
  Illinois Central
  Michigan Central
Chicago & North Western Pass. Terminal
  Chicago & North Western
Dearborn Station
  Atchison, Topeka & Santa Fe
  Chicago & Eastern Illinois
  Chicago & Western Indiana
  Chicago, Indianapolis & Louisville
  Erie
  Grand Trunk Western
  Wabash

Grand Central Station
  Baltimore & Ohio
  Baltimore & Ohio Chicago Terminal
  Chicago Great Western
  Minneapolis, St. Paul & Sault Ste. Marie
  Pere Marquette
La Salle St. Station
  Chicago, Rock Island & Pacific
  New York Central
  New York, Chicago & St. Louis
Union Station
  Chicago, Burlington & Quincy
  Chicago, Milwaukee, St. Paul & Pacific
  Chicago & Alton
  Pennsylvania

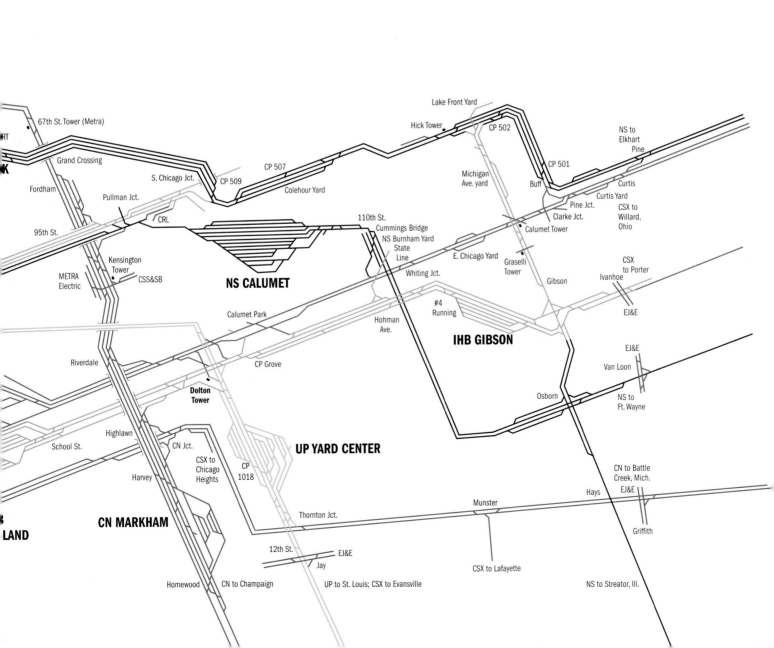

Above: Following Rock Island's 1975 bankruptcy, the railroad adopted a sky blue and white livery, but despite the optimistic colors the railroad was doomed to go out of business in 1980. In April 1978, a freight led by General Electric U33Bs with a road slug (for added traction) pass Blue Island. *Mike Abalos*; **Below:** In the 1970s, Rock Island was the sole user of La Salle Street Station, which was also its corporate headquarters. In addition to suburban services to Blue Island and Joliet, the Rock continued to operate its *Quad Cities Rocket* and *Peoria Rocket* until December 31, 1978. Rock's discontinuance of long-distance trains without regulatory approval went unchallenged. Less than a year later, in July 1979, the Rock was idled by a strike. After unsuccessful efforts to run the railroad with management personnel, the federal government stepped in to fund the railroad's revival for a brief period to move the 1979 harvest. RTA kept commuter trains running after the March 31, 1980, final shutdown. Rock Island Es, the mainstay of its ragtag passenger fleet, were being displaced by new RTA F40PHs when this picture was taken on October 24, 1977. *Mike Abalos*

The Rock Island declared bankruptcy in 1975 and shut down operations on March 31, 1980. Between Chicago and Mokena, its freight service was taken over by a downstate short line, the LaSalle & Bureau County, which renamed itself Chicago Rail Link in 1985. West of Joliet, where Metra ownership ends, Baltimore & Ohio bought the former Rock Island main line to Bureau, Illinois. In 1984 Iowa Interstate began operating the former Rock west of Bureau to Council Bluffs, Iowa, exercising trackage rights over B&O and Metra to reach the former Rock Burr Oak Yard in Blue Island.

On August 5, 1989, a shiny Soo Line GP38-2 leads the Chicago & North Western business train and two private cars north from Union Station on the former Milwaukee Road. The cars were part of a deadhead move (an empty equipment positioning move) to Canada for an American Association of Railroads special operated on Canadian Pacific. *Mike Abalos*

The Milwaukee Road entered bankruptcy in 1977 and was sold to Soo Line in 1985. This acquisition made the former Wisconsin Central superfluous, and Soo sold the former WC to a new company, Wisconsin Central Limited, effective October 11, 1987.

Chesapeake & Ohio and Baltimore & Ohio, operating under common ownership as Chessie System, merged at the holding company level with Seaboard Coast Line Industries, owner of Louisville & Nashville, on November 1, 1980, forming CSX Corporation. For more than five years

Samuel Insull bought the Chicago, Lake Shore & South Bend interurban electric in 1925 and renamed it Chicago South Shore & South Bend Railroad. Among his improvements was changing its overhead system from alternating current to direct current to make it compatible with Illinois Central's new electrification, allowing CSS&SB passenger trains to operate on IC to downtown. Electrics 1013 and 1012 lead a South Shore freight near Michigan City, Indiana in 1961. *Richard Jay Solomon*

Above: In January 1983, Conrail trains cross the massive lift bridge over the Calumet River near 95th Street. Historically, the Pennsylvania Railroad and New York Central lines ran parallel on their way east from Englewood to the Indiana border. After the Penn Central merger, a new connection in Hammond routed all trains onto the former PRR, and the NYC was abandoned. *Mike Abalos*; **Below:** The immense scale of transportation and industrial infrastructure south of Chicago overwhelms Conrail train BNELG-2 (Burlington Northern–Elkhart) on February 23, 1997, as it weaves eastbound near Hammond, Indiana. *Mike Abalos*

Chessie and the renamed Seaboard System operated independently, but beginning in 1986 the railroads were merged into CSX Transportation, which subsequently abandoned most of the C&O of Indiana. Baltimore & Ohio Chicago Terminal remains a separately operated CSXT subsidiary.

The federal government sold Conrail's stock in a 1987 public offering. Both Norfolk Southern (NS) and CSX were interested in buying Conrail, and after CSX struck a merger deal with Conrail management in 1996, a bidding war broke out. Ultimately NS and CSX agreed to purchase Conrail jointly; the two buyers divided Conrail between them on June 1, 1999. In Chicago, almost all Conrail trackage went to NS, with the exception of the former PRR Fort Wayne main line, which was assigned to CSX. CSX didn't keep it long, leasing the line east of Tolleston (Gary), Indiana, to RailAmerica

Left: In November 1985, a quartet of new Missouri Pacific C36-7s are ready for a late afternoon departure with symbol freight CFZ (Chicago Ft. Worth intermodal) from Yard Center (located south of Dolton). MP accessed Chicago via the western leg of the Chicago & Eastern Illinois. Although Union Pacific acquired it in 1982, MP retained its identity for a few years before it was assimilated into UP. It wasn't formally merged with UP until 1997. *Mike Abalos*;

Below: A Union Pacific passenger special (Symbol ZZRPK-12) and a commuter train depart the Chicago & North Western Terminal simultaneously on August 12, 1995. Both trains are passing though the Clinton Street interlocking that marks the split between the west and north/northwest corridors of Union Pacific's former C&NW lines; the latter route diverges to the north (just above the lead locomotive on the passenger special). *Mike Abalos*

On April 22, 2000, a BNSF transfer has just departed the east end of Cicero Yard and is pulling southbound onto Belt Railway of Chicago's main line (a connection known as the Hole). Waiting in the distance is Union Pacific train IHNCH-21 (Herington, Kansas to Chicago). At the time of the photograph, this UP freight used I&M RailLink's former Milwaukee Road route between Kansas City and Chicago. This routing was soon to change; by 2002 (when the aforesaid Kansas City line passed to Iowa, Chicago & Eastern) this train was accessing trackage rights over BNSF (former Santa Fe) from Kansas City to Chicago. *Chris Guss*

(now Genesee & Wyoming [G&W]) in 2004. G&W operates this property as the Chicago, Fort Wayne & Eastern.

Union Pacific first obtained direct access to Chicago when it merged with Missouri Pacific in 1982. Chicago & North Western, which served as UP's primary eastern connection, was acquired by an investment group including UP in 1989. UP sought authority to control C&NW in 1993 and, after its application was approved, it bought the North Western on April 25, 1995. A year later, UP merged with the Southern Pacific system, including SP's recently acquired East St. Louis–Joliet line.

Simultaneously, Burlington Northern and Santa Fe were implementing their merger, with the holding companies combining on

September 22, 1995 and the railroads merging at the end of 1996. As a condition of this consolidation, BNSF granted SP trackage rights over the Santa Fe main line between Chicago, Kansas City, and Hutchinson, Kansas, supplementing rights SP obtained over BN's Chicago–Kansas City line in 1990. UP obtained these rights through the SP merger.

Canadian Pacific, which controlled Soo Line, bought out minority stockholders in 1990 and began referring to Soo as CP (though Soo's corporate name hasn't been changed). I&M Rail Link bought Soo's former Milwaukee Road line west from Pingree Grove, Illinois (where Metra ownership of the former Chicago & Pacific ends), in 1997, and sold the property to Iowa, Chicago & Eastern Railroad in

Chicago was (and is) the great meeting point of eastern and western rail lines. On April 29, 1990, a Chicago & North Western loaded coal train led by SD50 7001 pulls into the small Grand Trunk Western Yard just south of the Blue Island interlocking. From here, the GTW will transport the coal to a power plant in Michigan. Indiana Harbor Belt's main line, with a New York Central–era signal bridge, is visible just above the third car in the train. *Mike Abalos*

2002. CP purchased IC&E parent Dakota, Minnesota & Eastern in 2008, returning IC&E routes to the CP system.

Similarly, Canadian National phased out the Grand Trunk Western trade name in the early 1990s, though GTW's formal corporate title remains the same. CN embarked on a major U.S. expansion following its 1995 privatization, acquiring Illinois Central in 1999 and Wisconsin Central in 2001.

Operations through Chicago had long been a headache for WC, so CN acquired Elgin, Joliet & Eastern in 2009 to link IC and WC.

A twenty-two-inch snowfall on New Year's Day 1999 practically shut down the Chicago terminal, and the embarrassed railroads began considering changes in their operations and facilities to avoid future service failures and improve the flow of traffic. After the federal, state, and city governments agreed to participate, this effort was branded the Chicago Region Environmental and Transportation Efficiency Project, or CREATE, when it was publicly announced in 2003. Under the CREATE program, government and railroad funds are being used to improve four railroad corridors through the Chicago area. The program includes construction of twenty-five new rail-highway grade separations, six grade separations at railroad level (diamond) crossings, thirty-six freight projects, and integration of area dispatching.

As of winter 2013–2014, seventeen of the forty-two planned CREATE projects had been completed. This included automation of Brighton Park in 2007, the last non-interlocked junction in the Chicago area, which had required all trains to stop before proceeding through the junction. Another major project is the flyover at Englewood, allowing Metra's Joliet Sub District (Rock Island) to pass over Norfolk Southern's Chicago Line (Fort Wayne). This improvement was scheduled to be completed by the end of 2014.

One of CREATE's largest infrastructure improvements is the grade crossing separation at Englewood. To eliminate congestion, this new installation will allow Metra's former Rock Island to fly over the former Pennsylvania Railroad Fort Wayne route (now Norfolk Southern's busy Chicago Line). This view of a southward Metra train from LaSalle Street Station to Joliet shows the project under construction in 2013. *Mark Llanuza*

CHAPTER 2

Chicago's Classic Passenger Terminals and Trains

By Brian Solomon

By virtue of Chicago's complex network and exceptional number of different carriers reaching the city, the railway traveler in downtown Chicago had a choice of more major passenger terminals than in any other American metropolis. Even today there are four primary terminals serving Chicago's suburban passengers.

Avid British railway traveler J. P. Pearson marveled at Chicago's stations in his 1932 book Railways and Scenery, noting after his 1912 visit "the chief glory of Chicago, however, in the way of railway depots, at the time of my visit, was the terminus of the Chicago and North Western line. . . . Built in 1911, it clearly ranks with the Pennsylvania Depot in New York and the Union Depot in Washington and is undoubtedly one of the finest stations in the world." Pearson's foreign eyes provide an excellent window on the past, when Chicago passenger railroading was in its golden age.

Chicago's disparate stations were a delight for railway enthusiasts and boon for the city's architectural heritage, but presented a challenge for travelers. When making connections between long-distance trains, travelers with a lot of luggage faced a daunting midjourney adventure navigating Chicago's downtown. One wonders how often a passenger stood pondering the departures board at Chicago's *Central* Station, when he should have been at *Grand* Central Station (not to be confused with New York City's famous terminal) or Union Station.

One man's problem is another's opportunity. For many years the difficulty of making connections between Chicago's termini was eased by the Parmelee Transfer Company service, which provided connections to all of the city's main stations, including interurban termini. For many through passengers the transfer (in the form of a voucher or coupon) was included in the price of their ticket. Founded by Frank Parmelee in the 1850s, the company began as a horse-drawn service using wagons and omnibuses, and by World War I had adopted motor vehicles. Though the Parmelee buses became famous, the firm lost its contract with the railroads to a competitor led by John L. Keeshin in 1955.

Opposite Page: A Milwaukee Road E-unit waits along Union Station's north platforms. (See page 90.) *John Gruber*

LaSalle Street Station

La Salle Street Station's origins were with Rock Island's first passenger station located south of the latter-day terminal at 22nd Street. This station served the Rock Island Railroad beginning in 1851, joined soon after by New York Central predecessor Northern Indiana Railroad. A far cry from the vast and elegant stations of later years, Rock Island's original station was described decades after its abandonment by valuation engineer Frank J. Nevins as "a plain wooden structure with board and batten walls, a shingle roof sixty-five feet long and twenty-five feet wide which enjoyed the luxury of coal-oil lamps and a clean coat of white wash!"

A new terminal was built at 12th Street in 1853, and by 1855, a more elaborate facility was established at LaSalle and Van Buren

Streets. This site served as a railway terminal continuously through 1981. In its early configuration the station head house was a framed brick building adjacent to a Howe truss shed spanning 116 feet over the platforms.

Continued traffic growth and rising prestige demanded further terminal improvement, so in 1868 an elegant station three stories high with impressive copper-topped mansard roofs was built. This featured an impressive truss train shed supported by massive limestone walls that spanned 186 feet across the station's twelve tracks. Less than three years after it opened, the station was destroyed in the Great Chicago Fire of October 1871. A similar structure was erected in the same place after the conflagration.

Construction of the classic LaSalle Street Station began in 1901, with the building opening on July 12, 1903. By that time, LaSalle

Nickel Plate Road's eastward *New Yorker* pauses at Englewood Union Station on a winter morning in 1959. Nickel Plate's Chicago trains provided a comfortable (though lightly patronized) alternative to New York Central's Water Level Route. Connecting with the Lackawanna at Buffalo, the *New Yorker* carried through sleepers and coaches to Hoboken, New Jersey (opposite Manhattan). *Richard Neumiller, courtesy of Bon French*

In 1971, many Penn Central locomotives still carried the lettering of their former owners. This PC train departs Union Station a week before Amtrak operations began. Prior to Amtrak, PC had largely consolidated its long-distance operations at Union Station, although a few former New York Central trains using the Big Four route continued to serve Central Station until 1972. *John Gruber*

Street was also serving Nickel Plate Road, then under Vanderbilt control as part of its extensive New York Central System.

Chicago & Eastern Illinois passenger trains also terminated here from 1904 through 1913, when these trains shifted back to Dearborn Street Station. The 1903 station featured a twelve-story office tower above the passenger facilities (where Rock Island and NYC kept offices) and direct above-street connections with the L. LaSalle served as the primary western terminus for New York Central's Great Steel Fleet. (Trains operating on the Big Four and Michigan Central [through 1958] ran to Central Station, rather than LaSalle Street.) Best known of the station's services was the *Twentieth Century Limited*, New York Central's exclusive, all-sleeper New York–Chicago express. Rock Island's trains included the

deluxe Chicago–Los Angeles *Golden State*, operated in cooperation with Southern Pacific.

The *Twentieth Century Limited* made its final runs in 1967, with the *Golden State* expiring the following year. Passenger trains on the Water Level Route were diverted to Union Station as a consequence of the 1968 Penn Central merger, yet LaSalle remained a long-distance terminal several years after Amtrak consolidated most long-distance services at Union Station. Rock Island didn't join Amtrak and continued operating its *Quad Cities Rocket* and *Peoria Rocket* until December 31, 1978. Rock Island was liquidated in 1980. The 1903 building was demolished in 1981, but a replacement LaSalle Street was built a block to the south, on Congress Street, as a terminal for Rock Island District passenger trains operated by Metra.

In addition to providing terminal facilities at Dearborn Station for a variety of roads, including Santa Fe, Erie, and Wabash, Chicago & Western Indiana also operated a limited suburban service on its 16.6 mile route to Dolton. On September 4, 1958, a Chicago & Western Indiana Alco RS-1 leads Dolton-bound train no. 66, which consists of former Erie Railroad Stillwell coaches. *Walter E. Zullig*

Dearborn Street Station

When considering Chicago's classic passenger terminals, Dearborn was one of the most interesting because of its archaic trackage and structures and its eclectic tenants. Dearborn's owner and operator, Chicago & Western Indiana, provided downtown terminal access and connections to a variety of Chicagoland latecomers. Dearborn served Chicago & Eastern Illinois; Erie Railroad; Grand Trunk Western; Monon; Wabash; and Atchison, Topeka & Santa Fe as well as C&WI's own commuter trains.

For the few years before Dearborn was finished in 1885, C&WI provided terminal facilities at temporary stations near Archer Avenue, then after 1882 in the vicinity of 12th and State Streets.

Typical of nineteenth-century stub terminal stations, Dearborn consisted of a head house, designed by Swiss-born Cyrus L. W. Eidlitz

(1853–1921), which faced Polk Street at ground level. This contained all the usual facilities: ticket offices, waiting rooms, and baggage areas on the ground floor with offices above. An expansive train shed covered an open concourse and the station's ten tracks and platforms beyond. As built, the shed was an unusual design of wrought iron and wooden construction that spanned 165 feet and extended 700 feet behind the station.

Dearborn was expanded with an annex to accommodate traffic growth. In the 1920s, its open concourse was finally enclosed. A fire in 1922 destroyed its steeply pitched roof and part of its iconic clock tower. After World War II, Dearborn was modernized when the railroads failed to build a proposed South Union Station intended to unify the secondary South Side railroad terminals.

C&WI compensated for Dearborn's limited platform space by employing a small army of switcher locomotives to keep the station fluid.

By the 1930s, Dearborn station was outmoded, and the city wanted to redevelop the property. But no money was available to implement any of the numerous station consolidation proposals, and Dearborn remained open until Amtrak. Dearborn's waiting room was modernized, though the Victorian-era shed survived, creating a stark contrast with postwar streamlined trains. Dearborn Station closed on May 2, 1971, after the final Santa Fe trains from California rolled to a stop. The front of the head house was preserved, but the rest of the property was finally redeveloped as the Dearborn Park neighborhood starting in 1977. *J. Michael Gruber collection*

No sooner than a train had arrived and emptied its passengers than a switcher would tie on to its back and take it out of the station, freeing a platform for another train.

Santa Fe, the only railroad serving Dearborn that wasn't a stakeholder in C&WI, was the last carrier offering more than token service. When Amtrak assumed long-distance passenger service in 1971, the surviving Santa Fe trains shifted to Union Station, and the last trains operated by Grand Trunk Western, Norfolk & Western, and Louisville & Nashville were discontinued. After Dearborn closed, N&W built a lone platform next to the station for its lone Orland Park commuter train. This train migrated to Union Station in December 1976. Efforts to preserve Dearborn's classic train shed failed, and it was demolished in May 1976 to make way for the new residential neighborhood known as Dearborn Park. The front of the old Dearborn head house was preserved in connection with this development.

By April 1968, Dearborn Station had lost many of its storied streamlines, but it remained a fascinating place to watch trains. In this view a Santa Fe Fairbanks-Morse switcher can be seen alongside Grand Trunk Western GP9s, a Chicago & Western Indiana RS-1, and Erie Lackawanna E8As. The station closed three years later after Amtrak took over. *Craig Willett*

Chicago & North Western Station

Chicago & North Western enjoyed a pioneering presence in Chicago by virtue of its oldest antecedent, Galena & Chicago Union Railroad. As C&NW assimilated predecessors and rapidly growing traffic, it needed to expand its Chicago passenger facilities on several occasions, with each new terminal replacing older ones.

To consolidate several older stations, C&NW built a central Chicago terminal at Wells and Kinzie Streets between 1881 and 1882. (A half-century later this became the site of Chicago's art deco icon, Merchandise Mart—deemed the world's largest building when it opened in 1930.) However, this facility couldn't keep pace with the swell of traffic. An article in the October 20, 1911, *Railway Age* said that by 1908 C&NW's Chicago terminal was handling an estimated three hundred weekday trains—any of which could be delayed when the bridge over the Chicago River opened for maritime traffic.

Construction of C&NW's new terminal building, designed by Chicago architects Frost & Granger, finally began in late 1908. North Western Station opened to the public June 4, 1911. More than just a passenger station, the new terminal was by far the busiest and most important facility on the whole railroad. It was a symbol of the company for passengers, shippers, and investors. The head house and train shed occupied four city blocks between Clinton and Canal Streets with its primary Beaux Arts, neo-Roman façade facing Madison Street. Three enormous arches, each containing five large bronze doors, served as gateways to the public entrance court. The exterior was faced with Maine granite and embellished with marble columns. The main waiting room followed the pattern of a vast Roman atrium with a barrel vault ceiling covered in ribbed terra cotta tiles, supported by green-tinted Greek Cippolino marble columns. The adjacent concourse led to a sixteen-track boarding area.

North Western Station's tracks were covered by a 265,800-square-foot Bush-style train shed. At the time the station was designed, the Bush shed was a recent innovation, developed by Lackawanna chief engineer Lincoln Bush for that railroad's Hoboken Terminal in New Jersey. It used a steel and concrete structure to protect passengers while allowing effluence from locomotives to escape into the atmosphere. C&NW Pacifics await departure from North Western Station in the early 1950s. *Philip A. Weibler*

Above: A C&NW Pacific blasts under the Lake Street L on a bright afternoon. Classic railway baggage carts line the platforms at North Western Station. It was necessary for large terminals to handle passenger baggage quickly and efficiently. Checked baggage was handled in separate cars normally positioned at the head end of trains. *Philip A. Weibler;* **Left:** *O. P. Jones collection*

North Western Station offered every convenience to its passengers. In addition to a fine restaurant adjacent to the waiting room, passengers could use telephones, a telegraph office, a baggage office, information desk, newsstand, barbershop, and public toilets. On the third floor, the railroad provided special facilities for women, including baths, a nurse's office, and tearooms. *Railway Age* highlighted the railroad's paternalistic benevolence, noting that C&NW's "facilities for hospital and emergency service . . . are very complete and furnished free of charge."

North Western Station provided special facilities for immigrants, including baths, a laundry, and a low-cost eatery. The likely purpose of these facilities was to minimize the need for immigrants to interface with businessmen and other domestic railway users. In a similar effort to separate traffic, C&NW provided a separate Washington

Street concourse for suburban travelers. It allowed them to exit platforms directly, without the need to transit the main station.

North Western Station was served by a completely new and purpose-built network of tracks, with five individual interlocking towers controlling train movements. Most important was Lake Street Tower, a three-story structure located near the elevated crossing of that street. This tower controlled the sixteen platform tracks, which funneled into a six-track throat (passing beneath the Lake Street L), which separated into four-track grade-separated lines at nearby Clinton Street Tower. The north line was elevated for a mile, and the west approach for nearly a mile and quarter. Constructing these new grade-separated approaches around and over the original G&CU route was among the most expensive phases of the entire terminal project.

North Western Station was the eastern terminus for the Overland Route, operating to

Above: The tail sign on this round-end observation car announces the departure of North Western's flagship train, the *400*, on its way to the Twin Cities. The *400* competed with Milwaukee Road's famous *Hiawatha* and Burlington's *Twin Zephyrs*. In its heyday, train *401* departed Chicago at 3:00 p.m., arriving at St. Paul six hours and fifteen minutes later. *Philip A. Weibler*; **Below:** North Western used its distinctive style of short-blade three-position semaphore. An inbound suburban train passes beneath a signal bridge festooned with semaphores, each governing movements on a corresponding track below. *Philip A. Weibler*

the Pacific Coast in conjunction with Union Pacific and Southern Pacific. Its famous trains included the *Overland Limited* and in later years the streamlined *City* trains, including the C&NW-UP-SP *City of San Francisco* and C&NW-UP *City of Portland* and *City of Los Angeles*. It was also the eastern terminus for Northern Pacific's *North Coast Limited* through 1918, and (in later years) Soo Line trains to western Canada. Among C&NW's late-era flagships were its *400*s, which connected Chicago and the Twin Cities in four hundred minutes.

In October 1955 Union Pacific shifted its Chicago passenger connection to the Milwaukee Road. C&NW exited the long-distance passenger business with the advent of Amtrak. Since that time, North Western Station has served exclusively as a suburban terminal. Unfortunately, the classic 1911 Frost & Granger head house was demolished in 1984 to make room for the postmodern Citicorp Center skyscraper. The terminal is now known as the Ogilvie Transportation Center, after Richard B. Ogilvie, a former governor of Illinois who supported the RTA's formation in the 1970s.

Chicago Union Station

Chicago had not enjoyed the benefit of a single unified long-distance passenger terminal along the lines of the Union Stations in Washington, D.C., Cincinnati, St. Louis, and Kansas City, to name just few. These terminals afforded passengers the convenience of one facility where all trains met, thus easing connections between trains and generally simplifying the process of travel. By virtue of the exceptional complexity of the rail network and parochial railroad interests, Chicago had six major downtown terminals until 1969. Compounding this confusion for the uninformed passenger was the fact that Chicago Union Station was never intended to function as an all-encompassing passenger terminal for the city's myriad passenger railroads.

Chicago Union Passenger Depot opened in 1882. Operated by Pennsylvania Railroad's Pittsburgh, Fort Wayne & Chicago subsidiary, it also served PRR's Panhandle Route; Chicago, Burlington & Quincy; Chicago, Milwaukee & St. Paul; and the Alton Route.

Unlike the other Chicago terminals, Union Station was arranged as a through station with lines feeding it from two sides. Despite this, the station in effect functioned as two back-to-back stub-end terminals because virtually

Above: In 1955, Union Pacific shifted its transcontinental passenger trains from its historic routing via Chicago & North Western to the Milwaukee Road east of Omaha. This August 1961 view shows an eastward UP-Milwaukee train, likely the Domeliner *City of Los Angeles*, approaching Chicago Union Station with UP E-units in the lead. The approaches to North Western Station, formerly the preferred route for UP's trains, can be seen to the left above the train. *Richard Jay Solomon;* **Below:** In contrast to the architectural elegance of its main waiting room and concourse, Chicago Union Station's boarding areas were dank and smoky—and that was before most of the train shed was buried beneath air-rights office buildings. In 1964, a Pennsylvania Railroad E-unit catches a wink of daylight in the closeted gloom of Union Station's platforms. *John Gruber*

every train arriving at the station terminated there. Located on the east side of Canal Street between Monroe and Adams Streets, the head house of the 1882 station was an elegant though not architecturally significant Victorian building.

Planning for a new Union Station began in 1910. A Chicago Union Station Company was formed in 1913, jointly owned by PRR's two subsidiaries, plus Burlington and Milwaukee Road. PRR was America's foremost railroad company, and although the other owners were involved, PRR clearly planned and directed

Left: A Milwaukee Road E-unit waits along Union Station's north platforms. The Milwaukee used the station's ten north tracks, while PRR, Alton/GM&O, and Burlington shared the fourteen south tracks. *John Gruber;* **Below:** Union Station's complex trackage facilitated parallel moves. In this 1964 view, Pennsylvania E8s lead an eastward train, while Gulf, Mobile & Ohio E7s depart with a train for the Alton route. By the mid-1960s, most passenger railroading had declined to a tawdry, tired condition that was a far cry from the elegance of the golden age. *John Gruber*

the project. PRR chief engineer Thomas Rodd was appointed chief engineer of Chicago Union Station Company, succeeded by Joshua d'Esposito in 1919. Graham, Anderson, Probst & White were retained as architects and executed designs inspired by Chicago architect Daniel Burnham.

Although a number of sites were investigated for the new Union Station, ultimately the railroads opted to remain near the 1882 station because of its proximity to Chicago's business district and the other main passenger stations. This required substantial expansion in very tight quarters. Enlargement of the passenger terminal required acquisition of adjacent property and relocation of freight facilities. U.S. involvement in World War I interrupted construction, and it wasn't until 1919 that work resumed. Complicating construction of the new station facilities was the necessity of keeping the old station in full operation without service interruption and with minimal inconvenience to passengers. As portions of the new station were completed and opened, older tracks and platforms were removed from service and demolished to make room for more new construction. Among the difficulties facing engineers was lowering the track level by an average of three to five feet.

The new Chicago Union Station finally opened in May 1925. It adopted an unusual arrangement whereby the station concourse and main station building occupied adjacent city blocks separated by Canal Street. Entrances were at street level, but tracks and most station facilities were located below street level, avoiding traffic conflicts. Cleverly integrated interior driveways allowed automobile traffic to reach the station without blocking the curbs.

The track arrangement was effectively twinned stub terminals arranged back to back with a few through tracks at the eastern edge of the station to allow for through moves and freight interchange. Pennsylvania's Fort Wayne Division trains, plus those of Burlington and Alton, served the south terminal tracks, and Milwaukee Road trains (and PRR Panhandle trains through about 1930) used the north tracks.

During a brief quiet moment, a railway worker relaxes on a baggage cart against a backdrop of Chicago's business district opposite the Chicago River. *John Gruber*

Among the most unusual aspects of the new station (largely out of sight from passengers) was its novel method of baggage distribution. Tracks were served by platforms on both sides—one for passengers, one for baggage and mail—with a below-platform baggage subway obviating the need for baggage elevators and speeding the movement of baggage to and from trains. A mail sorting facility opened over Union Station's south tracks in 1921 and became the world's largest post office when it was expanded in 1932, funneling mail to and from the trains below.

The concourse was similar to its counterpart in New York's Pennsylvania Station, strategically located between the ends of the north and south platforms. Steel lattice columns rose to support a high ceiling comprised of five parallel barrel vaults opening to skylights.

The main station housed waiting rooms and ticket offices, a lunch counter, barber, and other support facilities. The interior of the waiting room was bounded by Corinthian columns, with

the barrel vault ceiling rising 112 feet above the floor. At the center, an octagonal information booth was easily accessible from every direction. Outside, the Canal Street façade was lined with a classic Doric colonnade that established the building as a substantial railroad structure in the eyes of passengers. Located above the public station were railroad offices.

The classic concourse was demolished in 1966, replaced by a utilitarian facility under an air-rights office building. This concourse was rebuilt and improved in 1991. However, Union Station's original waiting room survives as the last classic railroad terminal in the city, and one of Chicago's great interior spaces. Union Station is Amtrak's Chicago hub and also serves Metra's BNSF, Milwaukee, North Central, Heritage, and Southwest Service lines.

Above: In June 1961, Gulf Mobile & Ohio's train no. 3, the *Abraham Lincoln*, bound for St. Louis, crosses the South Branch lift bridge south of Union Station. Bringing up the rear is a GM&O parlor observation lounge car. *Richard Jay Solomon;* **Below:** In January 1972, Milwaukee Road E9A 35A leads a rainbow consist on Amtrak's nameless train no. 324 southbound near Union Station. Amtrak's early trains offered an eclectic mix of equipment from different railroads. *George W. Kowanski*

Right: In Amtrak's formative years, a shortage of new equipment and the loss of domestic innovation led to an order for RTG TurboTrains from French manufacturer ANF. The first Turboliners were delivered October 1973 and assigned to Chicago–St. Louis runs. They were maintained at a new shop facility at Brighton Park. The Turbos later operated to Milwaukee, Detroit, and Port Huron, Michigan, before they were withdrawn in 1981, victims of their fixed consists and extravagant fuel consumption. One of the RTG Turbos passes 12th Street in September 1977. *Mike Abalos;* **Below:** In Amtrak's early years, its long-distance trains were hauled by inherited E and F units. These were mostly replaced with new EMD SDP40Fs in 1973–1974, but derailment problems with these units brought some of the streamlined veterans back until they could be replaced by F40PHs. Amtrak locomotives catch the afternoon sun at the former PRR 16th Street diesel shops near Union Station on October 5, 1975. *Mike Abalos*

Grand Central Station

Chicago's Grand Central Station is one of the city's most fascinating termini, the signature project of the virtually forgotten Chicago & Northern Pacific. Like one of the long-lost wonders of the ancient world, Grand Central was Chicago's finest passenger terminal in its heyday, applauded for its elegance. Designed by Solon S. Beman and built in 1890 on the former site of material yards and a prison, Grand Central boasted six station tracks under an arched train shed and a head house reminiscent of a Norman castle. The second largest clock in the United States topped the tower on the building's northeast corner. Aptly named, Grand Central was elegant, grand, and centrally located on West Harrison Street near Chicago's main business district. Its neoclassic interior was ornamented in high Victorian style with glided trim, Corinthian columns, and ample use of marble surfaces, which impressed many travelers in its early days. The station opened on December 8, 1890, and hosted through trains to the Pacific Northwest via Wisconsin Central and Northern Pacific. The NP system failed during the 1893 depression, and NP was forced to surrender control of both Wisconsin Central and C&NP on August 15 of that year. (Wisconsin Central would be

Although elegant, Chicago's Grand Central Station was never more than a minor terminal. It served Baltimore & Ohio, Pere Marquette, Soo Line, and Chicago Great Western. Unlike the other Chicago terminals, it didn't host significant suburban services. In 1913, Grand Central hosted just thirty-one daily trains, only about ten percent the number of North Western Station—Chicago's busiest at that time. When it closed in 1969, an average of only 210 passengers a day boarded or left trains there. *Philip A. Weibler*

This unusual view of Grand Central Station was made from its 247-feet high clock tower. We are looking down on the Victorian-era balloon-style train shed that covered six tracks. Between 1910 and 1947, various schemes for unifying Chicago's south-side stations envisioned phasing out Grand Central Station, but ultimately it was the decline of passenger service that doomed this terminal. *Philip A. Weibler*

leased by the Minneapolis, St. Paul & Sault Ste. Marie Railway, or Soo Line, in 1909.)

Grand Central slipped into relative obscurity even before its destruction, and in its later years it served four relatively minor passenger lines: Baltimore & Ohio (which bought the station in 1910), Pere Marquette, Chicago Great Western, and Soo Line (except for stints at Central Station in 1899–1914 and 1963–1965). In the 1960s it handled but a couple hundred passengers daily (compared with the thousands that passed through Chicago's busier termini). Today, the station's site is a grassy field, with virtually nothing left to remind us of what was once there.

J. P. Pearson offered a mixed opinion on his 1912 visit: "The Grand Central station . . . is very, though not specially, noteworthy (in 1893, I thought it the best station in Chicago). The façade, of dark red brick with a high tower

at one angle, had a good external aspect. The accommodations are placed near this angle of the building and include a very fine general waiting-room with striking pillars of polished yellow marble, very large and good windows of coloured [sic] glass and many seats. To right of this, on entering, are respectively the bookstall and ticket offices with, farther along, access to the 11 platforms lying off to the right, of which six are under a rather fine roof span."

By the late 1960s, the station was a ghost of its former glory. CGW, never a large passenger railroad, had ceased Chicago passenger operations in 1956. Soo's *Laker* had moved to Central Station in 1963 before expiring. And B&O/C&O were operating just a handful of trains. The station closed when B&O/C&O shifted their remaining services to North Western Station on November 8, 1969. Grand Central was demolished in 1971.

On November 8, 1969, Grand Central Station closed, and its last passenger tenants, Baltimore & Ohio and Chesapeake & Ohio, moved their trains to North Western Station. This arrangement lasted only eighteen months before all C&O and B&O trains serving Chicago were discontinued with Amtrak's implementation. On April 24, 1971, B&O's timetable eastbound *Capitol Limited* is seen on North Western heading west from downtown Chicago as the train begins its circuitous exit from the city. *John Gruber*

Central Station

Illinois Central's primary long-distance station was known to passengers as simply Central Station, scenically situated east of the Loop on the shore of Lake Michigan. Designed in the late Victorian Richardson Romanesque style by New York architect Bradford L. Gilbert, it opened on April 17, 1893, in anticipation of the World's Columbian Exposition held that year. For its time Central was an extraordinarily large station that included a nine-story office building and an imposing 225-foot clock tower.

New piling techniques were required to support the building on the marshy lakefront soil; the 610-foot-long train shed was the largest in the world at the time.

J. P. Pearson had found Central Station under construction during his visit in 1893, but was impressed with it on his return visit in 1912. Based on the later trip, he offered this qualified praise, in his characteristically verbose British prose: "The excellent Illinois Central depot on Lake and 12th Streets is also utilized by other roads . . . and has quite a good exterior with, however, rather a curious and awkward entrance (at least the one I went in by was so). The general waiting-room or booking hall . . . with its wide, low arched roof, lit up—a little garishly perhaps—by numbers of electric lamps, was extremely fine and spacious." Pearson was less impressed by the train shed, which he described as a "dingy ridge roof." The main "other roads" using Central Station included New York Central's Big Four and Michigan Central affiliates, and for brief periods, Wisconsin Central/Soo Line and Chesapeake & Ohio of Indiana trains.

As built, Central Station functioned as a through station rather than the stub-end variety, since IC's tracks continued north to Randolph Street. Because the station had through tracks, it could accommodate intensive overload capacity. The railroad's

C. H. Mottier explained in the book *Organization and Traffic of the Illinois Central System* (published in 1938) that on November 19, 1929, Central Station's eight tracks handled forty-three extra trains in addition to the seventy-eight trains normally scheduled to stop there. Once IC's suburban service was electrified, though, commuter trains bypassed Central Station, and it functioned as a terminal for through trains.

The coming of Amtrak doomed Central Station. Though Amtrak's former Illinois Central and Big Four route trains continued to operate into the station for nearly a year after the national carrier was formed, in March 1972 the switch was made to Union Station. Illinois Central Gulf offices vacated the premises a year later, and in 1974 the station was leveled.

On January 2, 1995, Amtrak's Chicago–Toronto *International* crossed the Rock Island at Englewood tower. At Englewood, where the Pennsylvania Railroad's Fort Wayne line met the Rock, the New York Central's one-time Lake Shore & Michigan Southern curved north to join the Rock for the last few miles to LaSalle Street Station. The *International* ran from 1982 to 2004 and routinely operated with VIA Rail locomotives. It was discontinued in April 2004 and replaced by the Chicago–Port Huron *Blue Water*. Reasons for discontinuing the *International* included border crossing delays and a relatively high cost of operation, combined with declining international ridership. Passenger rail activists decried loss of the *International* as a degradation of service. *Brian Solomon*

Sleepers, Streamliners, and Commuters

Chicago, where east meets west, was served by more railroads and more named luxury limiteds than any other city on the continent. Numerous carriers and ideal distances from several neighboring cities gave Chicago unparalleled competition as the railroads vying for passenger traffic tried to outdo each other in both performance and service.

The fiercest competition was between Chicago and New York, where America's largest railroads (also the nation's busiest passenger carriers) operated their finest trains. Pennsylvania Railroad and New York Central System made a show of topping one another with their premier services.

On June 15, 1902, the railroads simultaneously introduced their latest luxury fast trains on the Chicago–New York run: PRR's *Pennsylvania Special* (renamed the *Broadway Limited* a decade later) and New York Central's *Twentieth Century Limited*. A Chicago Tribune reporter on the inaugural eastward run of PRR's train wrote: "At Englewood, where a stop of one minute was made, the station platform was thronged with people, and their waving handkerchiefs made it look as if a cloud of white butterflies was just settling down upon them."

For years these premier limiteds were timed to simultaneously arrive and depart from Englewood to magnify the air of rivalry. Despite their widely differing routes, both lines offered nearly identical running times between end points, and over the years these were gradually tightened, necessitating fast running and careful timekeeping.

PRR and Central had the lion's share of traffic in this corridor, but they were not the only players. Baltimore & Ohio connected New York and Chicago by way of a roundabout route using

One of Pennsylvania Railroad's Loewy-streamlined T1 duplexes pauses with the westbound *Golden Arrow* (Detroit–Chicago Union Station) at Englewood in February 1947. Englewood Union Station served as a convenient suburban stop for long-distance passengers on Chicago's South Side. It was the first stop out of Chicago for many long-distance trains on the New York Central, Pennsylvania Railroad, and Rock Island Lines. *Jay Williams collection*

Above: A short eastward Penn Central passenger train carries a Flexi-Van intermodal car on the hind end. Flexi-Van was a New York Central innovation that allowed the railroad to carry intermodal shipments despite its tight clearances. PC phased out Flexi-Vans after the 1968 merger. Penn Central's application to discontinue all passenger trains west of Buffalo and Harrisburg was one key event spurring Congress to create Amtrak. *John Gruber;* **Bottom Left:** Baltimore & Ohio was Electro-Motive Corporation's first E-unit customer and the only railroad to buy the pioneering EA/EB E-unit models. On February 2, 1939, a B&O EA leads the *Capitol Limited* eastward against the backdrop of a hazy Chicago skyline. *J. Michael Gruber collection;* **Bottom Right:** In 1947, Erie Railroad served Chicago with three passenger roundtrips daily. Its flagship was the *Erie Limited*, and it also operated the *Midlander* and *Atlantic/Pacific Express*. Erie's trains served Dearborn Station. *Richard Solomon collection*

Great Northern's *Empire Builder* and Northern Pacific's *North Coast Limited* rest at Burlington's 14th Street Coach Yards south of Union Station. Though NP sent its premier trains to Chicago over Wisconsin Central and C&NW in earlier years, Burlington operated them from World War I through Amtrak, signifying GN and NP's fifty-fifty ownership of CB&Q from 1901 through the Burlington Northern merger in 1970. *Richard Jay Solomon*

the Reading and Central Railroad of New Jersey (plus a trans-Hudson bus ride) on the New York end. Erie Railroad also connected the dots via its scenic, if slow, route across New York's Southern Tier. Its famed *Erie Limited* provided adequate transportation, but never approached the levels of service operated by PRR and Central.

Chicago–St. Louis

Chicago and St. Louis were an ideal distance for a comfortable daytime railway journey or overnight train. Here several railroads competed for passenger business. On this route the Alton introduced George Pullman's first sleeping cars in 1859, setting a new standard for overnight service. By the 1890s, sleeping cars and diners were the norm on American long-distance trains. No fewer than four railroads fielded overnight trains on the Chicago–St. Louis route as late as 1949.

In the early years of the twentieth century, these lines offered some of America's finest "varnish"—as wooden-bodied long-distance trains were called because of their high gloss. Not only were the trains well appointed, comfortable, and stylish, but to distinguish their services from ordinary trains that used drab colors, typified by Pullman green, the railroads painted their passenger cars in brighter shades. In his book *Some Classic Trains*, Arthur Dubin noted that cars for Alton's flagship *Alton Limited* were painted a handsome deep red, while cars for Wabash's competing *Banner Blue Limited* were adorned in a royal blue with gold trim, and Illinois Central's *Daylight Special* (not to be confused with Southern Pacific's train of the same name) carried cars dressed in bright green from the windowsills to the roofline. Significantly, these colors carried over into the streamlined era and were adopted for early diesel paint liveries.

Transcontinental Connections

Of the roads from the far West, Santa Fe and Milwaukee Road served Chicago directly and provided through passenger trains to the coast. Santa Fe's route was one of the best, and its famous limiteds, such as the *California Limited*, *Grand Canyon*, and *Chief* were household names. Milwaukee's late-build transcontinental route was comparatively obscure, and its trains, such as the *Olympian*, less well known.

Other lines served as eastern connections for transcontinental routes. Burlington handled trains for its parent companies, Great Northern and Northern Pacific, as well as through services to the Bay Area using the Denver & Rio Grande Western/Western Pacific route. Chicago & North Western was the traditional eastern leg for Union Pacific/Southern Pacific Overland route trains, most famous in its day was the namesake *Overland Limited*. In 1955, UP had a falling out with C&NW and moved its Chicago trains to Milwaukee's route east of Omaha. Rock Island worked with Southern Pacific carrying trains via the Golden State route to southern California. The Soo Line was in Canadian Pacific's family and served as Chicago link for trains such as the *Soo-Pacific* and *Mountaineer* running to the Canadian Pacific Northwest, though the latter train was rerouted via the North Western east of St. Paul from 1933 through 1949.

Chicago at the Dawn of Streamlined Age

The streamlined train wasn't invented in Chicago, yet the city played a crucial role in the advent of this innovation. Events in the

Chicago & North Western serviced Union Pacific's *City* streamliners and other trains on the C&NW-UP-SP Overland Route. In 1936, the Pullman-built M-10001 assigned to *City of Portland* service rests at C&NW's Chicago Coach Yards. The gaping mouth-like grille gave these early streamliners an angry appearance. They were reportedly a nightmare to clean; dead birds and debris would collect in the engine compartment during their high-speed cross-country dashes. As a result, later trains featured air intakes on the sides. *Jay Williams collection*

In the late 1980s, EMD shifted locomotive production away from its LaGrange, Illinois, plant. Then in 2005, after seventy-five years under the wing of America's largest automobile manufacturer, EMD was sold to the investment consortium of Berkshire Partners and Greenbriar Equity Group, which renamed it Electro-Motive Diesel. Five years later Caterpillar acquired the builder, operating it under its Progress Rail subsidiary. Although its primary locomotive assembly plant is now in Muncie, Indiana, EMD's offices, locomotive test facilities, and engine plant remain at La Grange (McCook). EMD's main building was pictured in April 2013. *Tom Kline*

city focused on new technologies that made American streamlined trains possible, then as the new trains emerged, they basked in the Chicago spotlight. Chicago-based firms and railroads were among the foremost beneficiaries of their manufacture and operation.

By the early 1930s, railroads everywhere were facing declining passenger ridership. This decline was a result of improved public roads, rising private automobile ownership, and the budding airline and bus industries. Meanwhile, the Great Depression further reduced the numbers of people traveling by rail.

In 1933, Chicago's Century of Progress World's Fair was a sounding board for new ideas. Out of the ideas showcased at the Fair, a new paradigm for American passenger trains emerged, successfully brought to life by General Motors' Electro Motive Corporation

(using new engines developed by GM's Winton engine subsidiary). Key to the modern streamlined train was lightweight construction, aerodynamic styling, and power from compact, high-output internal combustion engines.

Both Union Pacific and Burlington hoped that sleek new trains would garner public attention and attract patronage back to the rails. Less obvious, but equally important, were lower operating costs afforded by greatly reducing train weight and taking advantage of better thermal efficiency and the reduced maintenance requirements of internal combustion power. Union Pacific worked with Pullman in development of an aluminum riveted train called the Streamliner, train M-10000, while Burlington and Budd joined forces in creation of a welded stainless steel train named the *Zephyr*. Although both trains were powered by

Winton engines, UP's Pullman-built train was ready before CB&Q's, and used a high-output, spark plug distillate engine instead of *Zephyr's* Winton 201A diesel.

The *Streamliner* and *Zephyr* toured America, setting new speed records and starring at the 1934 installment of the Century of Progress fair. These trains represented a real railroad success story, not only spawning fleets of diesel streamliners but also sparking major changes in the railroad industry that boosted Chicago-area railroad manufacturing.

By mid-1934, Union Pacific commissioned Pullman to build a second streamliner patterned after the first, the M-10001. It was famous for a lightning-fast demonstration in October 1934, running from Los Angeles to Chicago in thirty-eight hours and fifty-two minutes, at

one point reportedly hitting 120 miles per hour. On June 6, 1935, the M-10001 entered service between Chicago and Portland, Oregon, as the weekly *City of Portland*. On the Chicago end, it was serviced and maintained between runs at Chicago & North Western's facilities.

For all the flash of UP's early streamliners, it was Burlington's *Zephyr* that had the most lasting influence on American railroads. As a result of *Zephyr's* successful lightweight design, the welded stainless steel passenger car became a new American standard. (However, the articulation featured on the original Budd trains was found to be ineffective for widespread application, and so stainless steel cars with conventional types of wheel sets and couplers were adopted in later years.) Even more significant, the public success of

In June 1961, the *Denver Zephyr* departs Union Station. From the 1930s until Amtrak assumed long-distance operations in 1971, Burlington's flagship was the *Denver Zephyr*, and the railroad took great pride in operating this train with exceptional speed and efficiency. At peak times, Burlington operated the *Denver Zephyr* in multiple sections, with the first *Denver Zephyr* equipped with Pullman sleepers and second *Denver Zephyr* carrying coaches. *Richard Jay Solomon*

the *Zephyr* helped establish both the diesel-electric locomotive and its manufacturer—General Motors' EMC—as the new power for American rails.

Although in its railcar-producing period EMC had been a Cleveland-based engineering firm, when it made the transition to a full-fledged locomotive manufacturer, it established its primary factory near the Chicago suburb of La Grange—not far from Burlington's main line. (EMC's plant actually is in the tiny suburb of McCook, served by the La Grange post office.)

General Motors reorganized EMC as its Electro-Motive Division on January 1, 1941. By this time the company had introduced its mass-produced commercial models and was on its way to becoming America's foremost locomotive manufacturer, which allowed Chicago to outpace historic locomotive building centers in Philadelphia, Schenectady, New York, and Lima, Ohio. Burlington's original *Zephyr* has been beautifully preserved at the Chicago Museum of Science and Industry.

Streamliners Serve Chicago

Today it seems remarkable how quickly the streamlined train moved from futuristic concept to daily service. From their inception, Chicago was the best place to witness and ride streamlined trains.

On April 15, 1935, Burlington introduced a pair of EMC-powered Budd shovel-nose stainless steel articulated streamlined trains in daily service on its Mississippi River route between Chicago and the Twin Cities of Minneapolis–St. Paul as the *Twin Zephyrs*. Designed to bedazzle the public, Burlington hosted ample pomp and circumstance, dedicating the trains at Chicago Union Station by twin sisters Marion and Francis Beeler (as reported in *Trains* magazine, thirty years after the event).

Planning for this flashy new service contributed to a high-profile speed war with Milwaukee Road and Chicago & North Western. Burlington's similarly styled *Denver*

Burlington's *Denver Zephyr* made its debut in 1936. The original trains shared styling with the original *Pioneer Zephyr* and *Twin Cities Zephyrs*, using shovel-nose power cars and articulated stainless steel passenger cars. Although shovel-noses gave way to conventional E units in 1940, the Burlington bought whole fleets of stainless steel equipment through 1956 that personified its passenger services. *Vintage postcard, Richard Jay Solomon collection*

ONE OF THE STREAMLINED BURLINGTON ROUTE ZEPHYRS

On a clear morning in the summer of 1964, a westward Burlington streamliner, likely the *Morning Zephyr* for Minnesota's Twin Cities, is heading south from Union Station and will shortly swing west toward Aurora. Although Burlington pioneered the use of streamlined diesel trains using fixed articulated consists, operational limitations of these trains led CB&Q to invest in more flexible standardized equipment. *George Spier*

Zephyr made its debut in 1936, and over the next few decades whole fleets of stainless steel *Zephyrs* came to personify Burlington's passenger services.

Although the early trains were near copies of the articulated Budd prototype of 1934, the dramatic success of Burlington's *Zephyrs* demanded longer consists. By late 1936, standees on the *Twin Cities Zephyrs* forced Burlington to replace them with new seven-car trains, with the original consists shifted to the new *Nebraska Zephyr* service. Ultimately, the railroad shifted from articulated trainsets to individual cars with conventional couplers. Early Burlington passenger diesels emulated the shovel-nose design of the original articulated trains, but later trains were hauled by Electro-Motive E-units. Prewar, Burlington bought specially styled model E5s with fluted stainless steel embellishment. After the war, conventional

E7s, E8s, and E9s became the backbone of the passenger fleet. To improve locomotive utilization, Burlington rotated Es between intercity and suburban service, with eighteen locomotives typically required for Chicago–Aurora runs on weekdays. In the early 1950s, it was unusual for a railroad to run commuter trains with E units, as these locomotives were designed for long-distance runs.

Burlington's massive postwar investment in stainless steel passenger cars gave it the largest fleet of dome cars for its long-distance services. Best remembered was the 2,532-mile Chicago–Oakland *California Zephyr* operated in conjunction with Rio Grande and Western Pacific, which made its debut on March 20, 1949. For twenty-one years this train delighted passengers on its fifty hour thirty minute run across the West. It was one of the most popular trains of the streamlined era.

WRECK ON BURLINGTON'S TRIPLE TRACK CURTAILS SPEED

Ironically, Burlington, which had ushered in a new era of fast running in 1935, played a major role in bringing that era to a close. The railroad's triple-track raceway to Aurora was the scene of intensive activity. Between the various streamliners, long-haul passenger runs, suburban dinkies, and freight traffic, a train passed over the raceway every few minutes all day long. To cope with heavy traffic, Burlington had installed four-aspect automatic block signaling. Despite this protection, this section suffered one of the most disastrous wrecks in modern American history.

On April 25, 1946, Burlington's westward *Advance Flyer* had stopped on the main line near Naperville, Illinois, for an emergency equipment inspection when it was struck from behind at speed by the *Exposition Flyer* (heavyweight predecessor of the *California Zephyr*). When the dust settled, 45 people were dead and more than 120 seriously injured.

Following intensive investigation of the collision by the Interstate Commerce Commission (ICC, the government agency then tasked with railway accident investigation and safety enforcement), the ICC in 1947 issued new and more stringent train speed restrictions that affected all carriers across the country. Among the new rules was a 79-mile-per-hour speed limit on passenger trains operated in block signal territory unless protected by one of several forms of advanced signal protection.

This ruling anticipated a boom in implementation of advanced signal systems, but the result was quite different. Santa Fe and Union Pacific made major investments in advanced signals, but the high cost of signal systems, combined with low financial return from passenger services, discouraged most carriers from making the investment. Instead, they reduced their timetable speed limits to comply with the ICC order. With the advent of reliable jet aircraft, railroad passenger marketing focused more on comfort than speed. Some railroads continued to invest in passenger service through the 1960s, but the excitement of ever-faster running had faded.

Milwaukee Road's Hiawathas

Burlington and Union Pacific dabbled with internal combustion, but Milwaukee Road worked with Alco to refine exceptionally fast steam locomotives, initially in the form of 4-4-2 Atlantics, colorfully styled in aerodynamic shrouds. Meanwhile, its Milwaukee shops built a small fleet of very advanced lightweight passenger cars. These were combined for service on Milwaukee's new and fast Chicago–Milwaukee–Twin Cities service competing with Burlington's *Twin Zephyrs*. Public trials of the new equipment began on May 15, 1935, and revenue service was inaugurated two weeks later.

The trains were a phenomenal success, and Milwaukee soon added more cars and equipment while expanding its *Hiawatha* concept to other routes. Significantly, these are believed to have been the fastest regularly scheduled steam runs in the world. A small fleet of Otto Kuhler–styled 4-6-4s superseded the Atlantics in 1938, and diesels joined the high-speed fleet on the eve of World War II. In its heyday, the *Morning Hiawatha* was scheduled to make the eighty-five-mile sprint from Chicago Union Station to Milwaukee in 69.5 minutes. North of tower A-20 (20.3 miles from Union Station) to Lake (just south of Milwaukee), the *Hiawatha* sailed along at an average speed of 90 miles per hour. Yet even faster running was achieved beyond Milwaukee, where speeds exceeding 110 miles per hour were common. Milwaukee's fast steam was finally phased out in the early 1950s, by which time the streamlined Atlantics and Hudsons had been demoted to secondary service. Milwaukee's fast running was eventually slowed to 90 miles per hour following the ICC's 1947 ruling on high-speed services.

A new streamlined A1 4-4-2 Atlantic departs Chicago with Milwaukee Road's superfast *Hiawatha* in 1936. Four specially styled Atlantics were built by Alco for the *Hiawatha*, followed by a fleet of more powerful 4-6-4s streamlined by Otto Kuhler. The *Hiawathas* were among the fastest trains in America. *Seaver photo, Jay Williams collection*

the train its name. C&NW adopted the *400* brand for new passenger services over the next two decades. Diesels and streamlined equipment were first assigned to the original *400*s in 1939, and in 1941 C&NW introduced fifteen new streamlined *400*s, representing the new face of passenger transport.

Carrying out a deal with Wisconsin regulators, C&NW discontinued scores of local trains in 1958, while introducing deluxe bi-level gallery cars on *400* routes between Chicago, Green Bay, and points north. In 1963, after nearly twenty-nine years of service, C&NW discontinued its original Chicago–Twin Cities *400*s, and the rest of the fleet disappeared when Amtrak took over.

Illinois Central

Perhaps the most unusual looking day train of the prewar era was Illinois Central's EMC-powered, Pullman-built, aluminum-bodied and articulated Green Diamond on the daily Chicago–St. Louis run. This train bore a family resemblance to the early UP streamliners, beginning service on May 17, 1936.

Significant among early Illinois Central streamliners was the colorfully painted, diesel-hauled *City of Miami* operated in conjunction with southern roads that made a roundtrip every third day between its namesake and Chicago, beginning in 1940.

By that year, IC boasted that thirty of its named trains were averaging 60 miles per hour start to stop times as result of tightened schedules and fast main-line running. IC's investment in advanced signaling allowed it to keep its reputation as a fast passenger line after the ICC order of 1947.

Among IC's finest long-distance trains were its all-Pullman *Panama Limited* and *City*

North Western's *400s* Redefine Passenger Services

As CB&Q and Milwaukee Road were planning their streamlined services, C&NW beat them at their own game by introducing its tightly scheduled *400* in January 1935. A far cry from the streamlined trains being prepped for other runs, the *400* utilized conventional steam locomotives and heavyweight cars, yet by avoiding delays necessary for fancy new equipment, the train was first among the new, fast Twin Cities–Chicago services.

It covered 409 miles in seven hours—roughly 400 miles in 400 minutes—thus earning

Illinois Central's *Green Diamond* streamliner was a unique train. It was built by Pullman in 1936 and powered with an EMC Winton diesel. The train's essential design and styling was similar to Union Pacific's original 1934 M-10000 *Streamliner*. *Green Diamond* was IC's first streamlined train and made its scheduled debut on the Chicago and St. Louis run on May 17, 1936. The train was fast, making the 294-mile journey in just 295 minutes. *J. Michael Gruber collection*

of New Orleans runs, which connected Chicago and the Crescent City in style and comfort. The *Panama Limited* was a 1913 renaming of IC's *Chicago and New Orleans Limited* to reflect the completion of the Panama Canal. In May 1942, IC re-equipped the train with all-streamlined consists, making it one of the few such improvements implemented during the difficult World War II years. The *City of New Orleans*, inaugurated in 1947, ran the length of the IC between Chicago and New Orleans from daybreak to midnight each day.

Santa Fe Streamliners

Santa Fe was impressed by Burlington's Zephyr but wanted more than its cramped accommodations and short inflexible consist could offer, so the railroad worked with

Budd and Electro-Motive to design a diesel streamliner with best qualities of the Zephyr and conventional coupled trains. In the meantime, in May 1936, Santa Fe introduced a very fast, once-weekly, diesel-powered Super Chief using well-appointed conventional equipment between Chicago and Los Angeles. Westbound this train raced across the railroad in thirty hours and forty-five minutes.

Santa Fe's all-new streamlined *Super Chief* made its debut in May 1937. Supremely styled by Paul F. Cret, S. B. McDonald, and Santa Fe advertising executive Roger W. Birdseye, the new *Super Chief* melded traditional Southwestern motifs in a jazzy art deco style with interior décor inspired by Native American themes. Public reaction to this flashy streamliner was outstanding, and *Super Chief* styling came to define Santa Fe's corporate image over the next few decades. In its heyday,

Santa Fe displays its new streamliners at Dearborn Station in the mid-1930s. Between gleaming Electro-Motive E1 diesels is 4-6-4 3460—Santa Fe's only fully streamlined steam locomotive. In contrast with the red, yellow, silver, and black warbonnet scheme, the Blue Goose was dressed in a pastel two-tone blue and silver livery. *J. Michael Gruber collection*

the *Super Chief* was one of America's most famous trains, *the* choice of passage to the West Coast for Hollywood stars, political figures, and business travelers.

Following the success of the *Super Chief*, Santa Fe introduced a family of similar streamlined trains by buying new equipment for existing scheduled operations, such as the *Chief* (daily Chicago–Los Angeles), and introducing new trains, such as *El Capitan*.

Following World War II, Santa Fe continued its investment in streamlined trains and expanded services. The last new streamlined service was the *San Francisco Chief*, introduced in 1954 between Chicago and San Francisco. In 1956, Hi-Level streamlined cars were introduced on *El Capitan*. These were the inspiration for Amtrak's Superliner cars, developed as its standard long-distance passenger car for Western routes in the 1970s.

Above: Santa Fe Alco PA diesels lead train 123, the *Grand Canyon*, westbound from Chicago's Dearborn Station shortly after 11:00 a.m. on July 16, 1958. Dissatisfied with the performance of the Alcos on its premier trains, Santa Fe tended to assign them to lower-priority runs before their 1968 retirement. *Richard Jay Solomon;*
Right: The *Grand Canyon* offered Pullman sleeping car and chair car service between Chicago and Los Angeles. Although less prestigious than Santa Fe's *Chiefs*, the *Grand Canyon* was a well-patronized train. *Richard Jay Solomon*

The *Grand Canyon* wasn't Santa Fe's most glamorous train. It departed Dearborn just after noon and in later years ran with a mixed consist of heavyweight and streamlined equipment. This view from the 18th Street bridge shows the train on C&WI's line approaching 21st Street; Illinois Central's elevated tracks are swinging off to the right toward 16th Street Tower (just out of the picture). Of the three tracks, only the two on the far right remain. The area to the left of these tracks has been converted to Ping Tom Park, named after a community leader in nearby Chinatown. The St. Charles Air Line bridge is at top left; beyond it is B&OCT's bridge to Grand Central Station. *Richard Jay Solomon*

Rock Island Rockets

For Rock Island, the streamlined era was something of a Hollywood Cinderella story. Despite its chronic financial problems, the bankrupt railroad invested in superbly styled diesel-powered stainless streamliners, beginning in 1937 with its *Peoria Rocket*, which worked daily trips between LaSalle Street and its namesake city. Initially, the *Rockets* were powered by six custom-styled EMC model TA diesels.

Two decades after receiving its original lightweight equipment, Rock Island made an unusual late-era investment in General Motors' *Aerotrain* and a similarly styled *Talgo* lightweight set. Briefly operated in long-distance service, the comfort quality of these low–center of gravity lightweights was lacking, so they were demoted to Chicago–Joliet suburban work, where they remained until retirement to museums in 1966.

Monon F3As lead an outbound passenger train from Dearborn Station near the 21st Street Bridge in 1956. Monon's passenger livery was gray and scarlet with white trim (the colors of the University of Indiana); its freight scheme was black and gold (the colors of Purdue University). In practice, locomotives were mixed depending on the demands of service. *J. Michael Gruber collection*

Monon's Postwar Passenger Renaissance

Monon, which had struggled financially through the Great Depression and World War II, finally emerged from bankruptcy after the war with John W. Barriger III at its helm. Barriger aggressively modernized the railroad during his six-year presidency. He quickly placed orders for modern diesels, including EMD F3s for freight and passenger service.

Barriger believed that passenger service had a profitable future and re-equipped the railroad's passenger fleet economically. Instead of commissioning new streamlined cars, Monon invested in surplus U.S. Army hospital cars built for World War II, and he had these rebuilt into coaches, dining-parlor cars, and observation cars. Barriger expanded service and revived the railroad's traditional named trains as handsome Raymond Loewy–styled diesel-powered pocket streamliners. Loewy's skillful adaptation of Indiana University's red and gray as Monon's new passenger livery helped encourage local loyalty for the services.

The *Tippecanoe* was reintroduced on the Chicago–Indianapolis run as a morning departure in 1946, while the *Hoosier* made its streamlined debut in 1947 as an evening run. In February 1948, Monon's *Thoroughbred* was introduced on the 324-mile Chicago–Louisville route. This was briefly joined by an overnight sleeping car service called the *Bluegrass* (discontinued in 1949). The *Thoroughbred*

A Monon passenger train near Dearborn Station carries an old heavyweight baggage car, which despite postwar paint makes for a stark contrast with the streamlined F3A leading the train. *Richard Jay Solomon*

Above: Monon's *Thoroughbred* (Chicago–Louisville) survived longer than its other passenger trains. On the evening of September 1, 1965, train No. 5, the southward *Thoroughbred*, was photographed north of Oakdale in Chicago. The *Thoroughbred* made its final runs just two years later. *Walter E. Zullig;* **Below:** Chicago & Eastern Illinois' combined *Georgian-Hummingbird* works southward through Hamilton Park, Chicago, on September 8, 1960. CE&I handed this train to Louisville & Nashville at Evansville, Indiana. The train split at Nashville, Tennessee; the *Hummingbird* continued to New Orleans, the *Georgian* to Atlanta. *Walter E. Zullig*

survived the longest, and in the mid-1960s Monon even ordered a pair of high-hood Alco C-420s for the service, making it one of only a few Chicago-area railroads to buy second-generation passenger diesels. Monon's passenger service concluded when the final *Thoroughbred* pulled into the platforms at Dearborn Station on September 30, 1967.

Memorable Minor Streamliners

Pere Marquette flirted with streamlined passenger trains on the eve of its absorption by Chesapeake & Ohio in 1947. It had the distinction of placing the first postwar orders for new streamlined equipment in the form of stainless steel, fluted-side, Pullman-built coaches and diners hauled by Electro-Motive E7s. These entered service in 1946 between Detroit and Grand Rapids, later migrating to Chicago–Grand Rapids runs, and were noted for employing attractive young women as dining car waitresses.

Chicago & Eastern Illinois not only hosted long-distance streamlined consists from its connection with Louisville & Nashville, such as the Florida-bound *Dixie Flagler*, but also invested in streamlined equipment to run its own intraline services named after regional birds. Introduced in 1946, C&EI's four-car *Meadowlark* connected Chicago with Cypress, Illinois, while the six-car *Whippoorwill* ran to Evansville, Indiana.

Under the progressive administration of John W. Barriger III, Monon modernized and expanded its passenger service. Among its popular trains was the Chicago–Indianapolis daytime service called the *Tippecanoe*. On September 6, 1958, a matching passenger trainset led by an F3A departs Dearborn Street Station. Monon's postwar passenger livery was styled by Raymond Loewy, who cleverly incorporated the colors of Indiana University in the railroad's new scheme. *Walter E. Zullig*

Among the most elegant trains operated by Chicago's minor passenger railroads was another postwar avian-inspired streamliner, Wabash's *Blue Bird*. This popular train made its debut on February 26, 1950, inaugurating dome service on the Chicago–St. Louis run. As with many streamlined trains, the *Blue Bird* was about adding style and flair to the travel experience to entice passengers to the rails. The interior of the train featured specially commissioned murals by Auriel Bessemer that illustrated historical and contemporary themes along the Wabash route.

In June 1961, Richard Solomon was afforded a cab ride on Chicago & Western Indiana RS-1 259 working toward Dolton with one of C&WI's commuter trains, which would be dropped in 1964. This view was made north of Dolton passing C&EI's Chicago-bound *Meadowlark*. C&EI introduced the *Meadowlark* (Chicago–Cypress, Illinois) in 1946, but between 1955 and 1962 this train operated using C&EI's lone Budd RDC—rare equipment in the Chicago area. *Richard Jay Solomon*

On July 21, 1958, the photographer held tickets for St. Louis as he snapped a photo boarding the Wabash Blue Bird under the shed at Dearborn Street with a Monon F3A on an adjacent track. Typically running with one or two Vista Domes, including a superb dome-parlor-observation at the rear, the *Blue Bird* flashed 286 miles over the Wabash for a late evening arrival in St. Louis. *Richard Jay Solomon*

Commuter Trains

Chicago was unique among Midwestern cities for its extensive and intensive suburban services, which were on par with those developed by railroads serving East Coast metropolitan centers. In 1913 B. J. Arnold, in his study of Chicago's terminals, estimated that Chicago suburban traffic accounted for about 42 million passengers annually.

First and foremost among Chicago's suburban railways was Illinois Central's north-south line running via Kensington and Harvey toward Homewood. It was significant not only for emerging as Chicago's most heavily traveled line and the busiest and most important Illinois Central passenger operation, but also for its pioneering use of steel-framed passenger cars in 1904, and later as the only Chicago-area heavy steam railway to be electrified. IC suburban operations included short branches to Blue Island and South Chicago, complementing the north-south trunk.

Rock Island developed its early suburban route via Englewood and Blue Island, ultimately extending service to Joliet at

In 1961, Richard Solomon made this photo of an Illinois Central electric commuter train on the South Chicago Branch from the top of an apartment building. Electrified in 1926, IC by 1929 had amassed a fleet of 280 cars (powered cars and trailers) to work a schedule of 542 weekday trains that carried an estimated 121,000 daily passengers. In this view, notice the unpowered trailer is leading. *Richard Jay Solomon*

On the evening of June 11, 2013, a Chicago-bound Metra Electric train pauses at South Shore Station on the South Chicago Branch. South Shore Station is located on South Exchange Avenue, a couple of blocks from the Lake Michigan shore. Although the station shares a name with the famous former Insull Interurban, it has no connection with it. *Brian Solomon*

the outer fringes of Chicago's commuter belt. Milwaukee Road operated significant commuter operations north and west from Union Station.

Among Chicago's classiest suburban lines was CB&Q's thirty-eight-mile main line to Aurora. In 1949, CB&Q ordered the first stainless steel bi-level gallery cars from Budd for its Chicago–Aurora dinkies. These cars featured central low-level double doors to allow rapid loading and unloading, with fifty-two single seats on the gallery level and 96 seats

below. Delivered in 1950, Burlington's gallery cars set the new standard for Chicago suburban service, eventually emulated by most of the region's commuter railroads.

Chicago & North Western was among the city's important suburban players and developed commuter services westward on its West Line to West Chicago and Geneva, its Northwest Line to the relatively distant points of Harvard and Williams Bay, Wisconsin, and its North Line to Kenosha, Wisconsin. C&NW's first gallery cars were built by St. Louis Car

Company. Delivered in 1955, these early cars were sometimes pulled by steam locomotives before steam was withdrawn from service the following year. Later orders built by Pullman-Standard were equipped for push-pull service, which C&NW introduced to the city. C&NW was also among the first to employ modern head-end heating and lighting technology, which set new standards for suburban operations.

Left: Rock Island was an unusual case. It was too broke to join Amtrak, and both its suburban services and a vestige of its long-distance service survived under traditional unified management longer than most other places in the United States. The *Quad Cities Rocket* and *Peoria Rocket* expired at the end of 1978. In this view, outbound suburban train 223 departs LaSalle Street Station at 5:16 p.m. on September 10, 1971. *George W. Kowanski;* **Below:** In 1955, Union Pacific shifted its eastward passenger connection from Chicago & North Western to Milwaukee Road, and as a result Milwaukee adopted UP's Armour Yellow and Harbor Mist Grey as its passenger livery. In June 1961, Milwaukee Road E9A 36 leads an afternoon suburban train north from Union Station. The Chicago River is to the left of the train. *Richard Jay Solomon*

Top Right: *O. P. Jones collection;* **Above:** C&NW Pacific 574 leads a suburban train while new EMD F-units work one of the railroad's *400* streamliners. This low angle view shows the unusual electric semaphore dwarf signals that were a signature of North Western's Chicago terminal. These are a variation of General Railway Signal's Type 2a semaphore. C&NW's use of steam locomotives in commuter service ended in 1956. *Philip A. Weibler;* **Below:** Where North Western Station's high signals used C&NW's unique adaptation of the General Railway Signal three-aspect semaphore blade, its low signals used a specially designed variant of GRS's two-aspect dwarf semaphore. These unusual dwarf semaphores dotted the approaches to the station until they were removed in the 2000s. A Metra train is inbound on December 18, 1994. *Brian Solomon*

CHAPTER 3

Chicago's Visual and Historic Legacy

By John Gruber

Chicago is often thought of as a rough-and-tumble railroad center, the "hog butcher of the world" in Carl Sandburg's 1913 poem, which also calls the city a "player with railroads and the nation's freight handler."

But after a look at its significant visual legacy, another and more creative image emerges from the shadows. The city's art and photography community recorded this legacy through travel posters, magnificent photographs, and a major exhibition at the Chicago History Museum. It encompasses a broad spectrum of the cityscape, including architecture and landscape architecture.

As the first railroad construction started, illustrations of the railroad scene started to appear. The Galena & Chicago Union's first steam locomotive, the *Pioneer*, went into service on October 10, 1848. It was preserved and moved around the city, and since 1972 has been on display at the Chicago History Museum.

Opposite Page: Sketch of two C&NW passenger trains by Alfred W. Johnson. (See page 134.) *John Gruber collection*

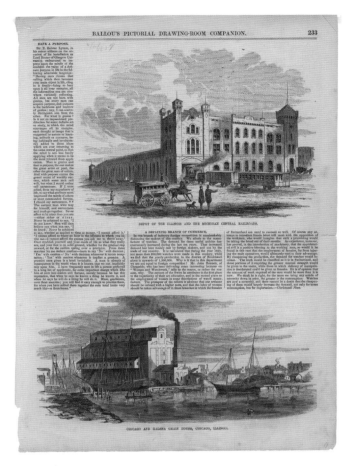

DEPOT OF THE ILLINOIS AND THE MICHIGAN CENTRAL RAILROADS.

CHICAGO AND GALENA GRAIN HOUSE, CHICAGO, ILLINOIS.

Stations, especially the Great Central Station on the lakefront, became a popular subject for photographers. For the printing press, photographs had to be converted to woodcuts or steel engravings. Such images were reproduced in *Chicago Illustrated: 1830–1866, Frank Leslie's Illustrated Newspaper, Daily Graphic: An Illustrated Evening Newspaper, Illustrated London News,* and *Ballou's Pictorial Drawing-Room Companion.*

Surprisingly, amateurs were involved from the early times. The Amateur Photographic Exchange Club, which existed only from 1861 to 1863 in Philadelphia, called for members to distribute their prints to all other members; a stereo view of the IC depot by a Philadelphia photographer was among the prints exchanged.

John Carbutt's studio and others produced railroad photographs. Carbutt (1832–1905) established his Garden City Photographic Art Gallery in Chicago in 1861, photographing Lincoln's funeral car in 1865, plus the Union Pacific's one hundredth meridian celebration in 1866, and Chicago & North Western's grand excursion to Upper Michigan in

Above: Woodcuts of the Illinois Central and Michigan Central Station on the lakefront were popular. This example is from an 1857 issue of *Ballou's Pictorial Drawing-Room Companion* published in Boston, Massachusetts. *Donnelley and Lee Library, Lake Forest College;* **Below:** An amateur, S. Fisher Corlies (1830–1888), made this stereo view of the Illinois Central and Michigan Central Station along the lakefront in 1863. He distributed it through the Amateur Photographic Club of Philadelphia. *Library of Congress, LC-DIG-stereo-1s01449*

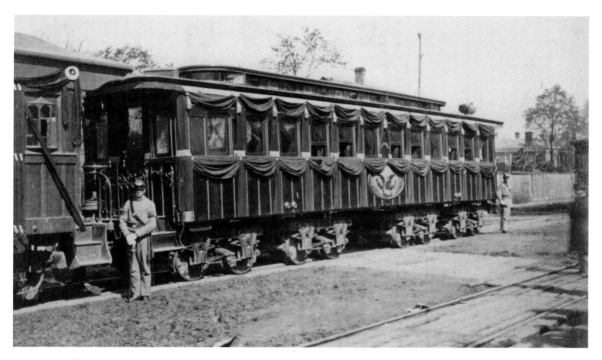

Above: John Carbutt photographed Lincoln's funeral train when it passed through Illinois in 1865. Carbutt's studio, located in Chicago from 1861 to 1871, produced work for Union Pacific and Chicago & North Western. *Donnelley and Lee Library, Lake Forest College*; **Below:** Carefully landscaped lawns spread across the front of the main shops of the Pullman Palace Car Company at Pullman, Illinois, about 1900. The Detroit Publishing Company, managed by William Henry Jackson, distributed the photo. *Library of Congress, LC-D4-10458 L*

1867. He moved to Philadelphia in 1871 to manufacture dry plates.

In 1881, George M. Pullman (1831–1897) opened an industrial complex to build railroad passenger and freight cars, including a town for its workers. (See Chapter 1.) Architect Solon S. Beman (1853–1914) and landscape architect Nathan F. Barrett (1845–1919) designed the factory buildings and grounds to be utilitarian and aesthetically pleasing, in keeping with Pullman's belief that environment was a crucial force in shaping workers' character. The water tower and shop's entrance formed the centerpiece of the company-owned town planned under Pullman's direction, with workers' residences, church, market, and recreational facilities.

Pullman's concept of a model town for his workers proved unsuccessful, but the company continued to build railroad cars on the site until 1982. A long list of photographers served the company: Thomas S. Johnson, Henry R.

Koopman, Wylie Dennison, John P. Van Vorst (the longest tenure of any, forty-one years), Clayton F. Smith, Joseph McAllister, Melvin C. Horn, Ernie Stutkus, Tom Considine, Donald J. O'Barski, and John Kniola.

Although three amateurs traveled on the Baltimore & Ohio's artist's and photographer's excursion in 1858, amateur photography did not become widespread until George Eastman announced the Kodak camera in 1888 with the advertising slogan, "You press the button and we do the rest." The camera and the film were sent back to Rochester for developing. The company introduced daylight loading film in 1891 and a pocket Kodak in 1895. Chicagoans began to document every aspect of their lives.

After the 1890s, the introduction of halftone and other photomechanical printing methods and high-speed printing presses allowed photographs to be published easily and cheaply. A new type of commercial photographer evolved for this market. Chicago became a major printing and publishing center in the West.

Fairs and Expositions

Fairs and expositions created opportunities for photographers, both for exhibition and for documenting the extravaganzas.

The National Exposition of Railway Appliances in 1883 featured the John Bull, built in 1831, C&NW's Pioneer, and four other locomotives. It was the Pioneer's first public appearance as a display locomotive. From this time, its future as a preserved locomotive seemed secure.

The World's Columbian Exposition in 1893 featured extensive railroad displays, including photographs by William Rau for the Pennsylvania Railroad and William Henry Jackson for the Baltimore & Ohio. The John Bull ran under its own power from Jersey City. Ida Hewitt Jones (1861–1953) came from West Virginia to operate the first train on the opening day of the exposition.

The Museum of Science and Industry opened in 1933 in a magnificent building built for the 1893 exposition. The museum is known

A Photochrom view shows the Field Columbian Museum at Jackson Park about 1901. The magnificent structure was built for the 1893 World's Columbian Exposition. Today the building houses the Museum of Science and Industry. *Library of Congress, LC-DIG-ppmsca-18167*

The Chicago & North Western celebrated the one hundredth anniversary of the Pioneer's first run and commemorated that centennial in 1948. Its company photographer, Donald S. Lidikey, documented the events—a press party for the centennial and the closing scene of the pageant at the Chicago Railroad Fair. *John Gruber collection*

for its historical and model railroad exhibits, most recently 2002's "The Great Train Story," a 3,500-square-foot HO-scale layout sponsored by BNSF that features more than thirty trains racing along 1,400 feet of track on a cross-country trip between Chicago and Seattle.

The 1933–1934 exposition, A Century of Progress, featured Edward Hungerford's pageant "Wings of a Century: the Romance of Transportation." The Burlington's dawn-to-dusk run of its new *Zephyr* train from Denver ended at the exposition in 1934.

The Chicago Railroad Fair in 1948 and 1949 celebrated one hundred years of Chicago railroad history. Thirty-nine railroad companies participated in the event along the shore of Lake Michigan. The "Wheels A-Rolling" pageant, also orchestrated by Hungerford, was a highlight. It is an example of what was possible when railroad corporate headquarters were in Chicago. C&NW marked the one hundredth anniversary of the Pioneer's first run and its company photographer, Donald S. Lidikey (1916–1997), documented the event.

Commercial Photography

Chicago, as the nation's rail center, attracted commercial photographers serving railroads. Unlike the early studio photographers who concentrated on portraits, these later photographers focused on architecture and advertising work. Although passenger travel always got the most attention, Chicago's role as a freight center also produced creative views.

William Henry Jackson visited Chicago in a photo car in 1898 as a part of his travels for the Chicago & North Western and Detroit Publishing Company. His work symbolized the role of photography in promoting railroad travel. During this Detroit period, many of Jackson's earlier and contemporary black-and-white negatives were converted to Photochrom, a Swiss photomechanical process that enabled mass production of vivid color prints. Each color in the final print required a separate asphalt-coated lithographic stone; usually at least six and often more than ten stones were needed.

Above: The Detroit Publishing Company distributed color views using its exclusive Photochrom process. William Henry Jackson was in Chicago more than once to make photographs. Here, about 1900, is the river in Chicago with elevators for the Chicago Railway Terminal and Rock Island. *Library of Congress, LC-DIG-ppmsca-18101;*
Bottom Left: George R. Lawrence, using the world's largest camera, made a large-format portrait in 1900 of the Chicago & Alton's newest train, its six-car Alton Limited. Lawrence set up the twenty-foot-long camera at Brighton Park, making his exposure on a 59x96Ð plate. The camera was dismantled a few years later. *Donnelley and Lee Library, Lake Forest College*

In 1900, George R. Lawrence (1867–1938), using the world's largest camera, made a large format portrait of the Chicago & Alton's newest train, its six-car Alton Limited. Lawrence set up the twenty-foot long camera at Brighton Park, making his exposure on a 59 × 96" plate and developing it later that day in Chicago. Prints were exhibited at the 1900 Paris Exposition. "The stir which the immense picture created in Paris is shown by the fact that affidavits were required before the Exposition officials consented to label the exhibit the largest photograph ever made on one piece," said *Scientific American*.

Jackson's son, Clarence S. Jackson (1876–1961), was official photographer for the Alton from 1901 to 1905, attached to the passenger department. As might be expected, his attractive views along the line were used for lectures and advertisements. But his principal work for the engineering and mechanical departments was "as a substitute for written reports, whenever possible," according to *World's Work*, a magazine published in New York City. "The photographs tell what has been done better than any written description, and they constitute a continuous record of the progress made in structural undertakings."

Kaufmann & Fabry (K&F), successor to George R. Lawrence's company in 1910, had more than a dozen railroad clients, including Illinois Central, Santa Fe, Union Pacific,

Pennsylvania, and Chicago & Eastern Illinois. "Pictures were received from all over the country on behalf of these railroads to be enlarged and hand colored. They were used for advertising and décor in the home offices," said Michael A. Kleiman, president of K&S Photographics, in 1997. His father, David Kleiman, had purchased Kaufmann & Fabry and merged it into K&S Photographics in 1965.

K&F photographers were active for many years. In 1937, Illinois Central posed "The Five Titans," five steam locomotives lined up at night with downtown Chicago in the background, to promote its fast merchandise trains pulling out of Congress Street Yard every evening. The Kaufmann & Fabry photo by Adolph Pressler appeared first in the Saturday Photogravure section of the *Chicago Daily News* with the headline, "Expressing the Spirit of Chicago and Renewing Romance of the Rails." IC also maintained its staff of photographers: John K. Melton, Henry H. Gilbson, Luther Paul, Elvis R. Adams, and O'Barski.

Hedrich-Blessing, a leader in architectural and industrial photography founded in 1929, extensively served three large railroads, Chicago, Burlington & Quincy, Great Northern, and Illinois Central, plus (not as frequently) Rock Island and Union Pacific. After seeing Ken Hedrich's work at Chicago's Century of Progress in 1933, the Burlington sent him on tour with the first *Zephyr* streamlined train. Hedrich and

Kaufmann, Weimer & Fabry, famous for panoramas, produced this bird's-eye view of Chicago in 1912. Weimer was associated with the company for only a short time. *Library of Congress, LC-DIG-ds-03626*

Illinois Central lined up five steam locomotives at night with downtown Chicago in the background to promote its fast merchandise trains pulling out of Congress Street Yard every evening. Adolph Pressler made the photograph for Kaufmann & Fabry. *John Gruber collection*

Bob Harr photographed along the GN in the 1950s. CB&Q sandwiched two of its negatives to show its new *Denver Zephyr* on the triple-track suburban line near Chicago in 1956 with the mountains of Montana in the background.

Torkel Korling (1903–1998) was among the independent commercial photographers serving railroads, especially Milwaukee Road, Chicago & North Western, and Pullman Company. In the 1930s, *Life* and *Fortune* frequently published his photos. "Here's How a Pullman Car Works" (*Carbuilder*, November 1946) featured a photo essay, writing that "the 'how' of mass production becomes a thing of beauty, as seen by the camera of Torkel Korling, one of America's foremost industrial photographers."

After King D. Ganaway (1883–1944), an African American butler in Chicago, won first prize in the fifteenth annual exhibition in 1921 at Wanamaker's Department Store in Philadelphia for "Spirit of Transportation," a photograph showing two sections of the *20th Century Limited* at the station, he worked for the *Chicago Bee* and set up the Chicago Bureau Art Studio. The photograph was reproduced many times, including in the *Santa Fe Magazine*.

A Depression-era promotion, *Railroad Week*, sponsored by the western railroads, ended with a parade through the Loop of fifteen thousand employees of ten western railroads and the Pullman Company in 1935. The railroads lined up their newest high-speed streamlined passenger trains, initially serving the Twin Cities and St. Louis, with a historic steam locomotive for a publicity photo. The event continued in

Above: King D. Ganaway's prize-winning photograph of two sections of the *20th Century Limited* in 1918 in Chicago enabled him to make a career change—from a butler to a photographer for the *Chicago Bee* and owner of the Chicago Bureau Art Studio. Fort Dearborn Magazine, *John Gruber collection;* **Below:** Torkel Korling, a Chicago industrial photographer who also was published in *Life* magazine, made this unusual view of Bensenville Yard for the Milwaukee Road in 1945. *John Gruber collection*

1936. The North Shore Line's *Electroliner* joined the high-speed fleet in 1941.

George Krambles and Wilbourne Cox, another professional colleague and fan, preserved the work of Albert F. Scholz's Logan Square Studios (company photographer for many of the Insull electric railways) when they bought the studio in 1940.

A Chicago publication inaugurated in 1944, *Negro Traveler*, made an unusual use of publicity photos. Rather than promoting passenger services, its editors, Clarence E. Markham (1911–1995) and his wife, Olga, published the photos "to create a greater sense of pride" among African Americans working on the trains. For example, for the tenth anniversary of the C&NW's fast *400*, the *Traveler* in its March 1945 issue used eight photos with full names in the captions.

To promote *Railroad Week* in 1935, Chicago railroads posed five locomotives on Burlington tracks near Halsted Street: a historic CB&Q steam locomotive and fast-running locomotives of the Milwaukee Road, North Western, and CB&Q, competitors on the Chicago to Twin Cities run; and the Alton from Chicago to St. Louis. *John Gruber collection*

With the transfer of long-distance passenger services to Amtrak in 1971 and a gradual reduction in public relations activities, company photographic activities were curtailed or moved out of the city as corporate headquarters moved. But Norfolk Southern has reestablished the position and sends its photographer to Chicago.

Documentary Photography

Chicago was the focus of the best overall portrait of railroading and its people and culture in the United States. This portrait was created by Jack Delano (1914–1997) in 1942 and 1943 as part of an assignment to document the nation's railroad story for the Farm Security Administration (FSA) Office of War Information. In his autobiography, he described the experience as "the most exciting part of the work I did for the OWI."

Delano also photographed infrastructure and rolling stock, but he concentrated on the people who worked on the railroads. Roy E. Stryker (1893–1975), head of the photography unit for both FSA and its successor OWI, instructed Delano to document in pictures the importance of the railroad industry during wartime and the contributions made by railroaders and their families to World War II on the home front. His images feature such scenes as children collecting salvaged metal for recycling into war materiel, posters in public and private places promoting the sale of war bonds, and the ever-present flags that honored service men and women. He spent a couple of days with the family of Indiana Harbor Belt conductor Daniel Sinise in Blue Island. Sinise's grandson, television actor Gary Sinise, keeps his

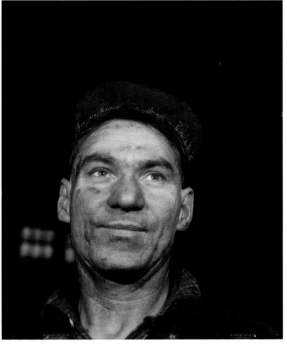

Jack Delano's extensive coverage of Chicago railroads in 1942 and 1943 produced a striking portfolio of railroads and their workers. Two photos on the C&NW's show a young worker at the 40th Street shops, and **(right)** Roy Nelin, a box packer in the roundhouse at Proviso Yard. The downtown skyline dominates a view of Illinois Central freight cars at its South Water Street freight terminal. The C&O and Nickel Plate railroads leased part of this terminal from the IC. *Library of Congress*

grandfather's railroad watch under a glass dome on his mantel.

Delano set out on his assignment with a full set of credentials from the FBI, Association of American Railroads, Headquarters of the Western Command, and War Department Office of the Chief of Transportation. It was a whole new world for Delano as he learned the language of the railroaders, such as *reefer* for refrigerator car or *highball* to start the train.

Delano wrote about the difficulties of the Chicago assignment, "the extensive arrangements and formalities, tho [sic] unavoidable, which take up so much time." And, he added, tongue-in-cheek, when "the great picture-taking day has finally come, I am just as likely to encounter fog, snow, sleet, or an eclipse of the sun."

Delano set a demanding schedule. He started the railroad project in November 1942, concentrating on the Indiana Harbor Belt, Illinois Central, Chicago Union Station, and Proviso Yard. It was interrupted by a trip to Minneapolis, Minnesota, and Madison, Wisconsin, then resumed with a month in March spent riding freight trains and visiting repair shops on the Santa Fe from Chicago to California. It concluded in May 1943 with coverage of the Rock Island in Blue Island and Milwaukee Road at Bensenville and Galewood.

Railroaders: Jack Delano's Homefront Photography, an exhibition created by the Center for Railroad Photography & Art in collaboration with the Chicago History Museum, demonstrates that the railroad industry—like ethnic, religious, and neighborhood enclaves—fostered its own communities and networks that cut across ethnic and religious lines. Through the stories of the lives of the men and women of railroading, an exhibition, catalog/book, and programs and publications demonstrate how the people of one industrial community represent, in microcosm, the vastness of Chicago society and, by extension, American society as a whole. The exhibition at the Chicago History Museum opened on April 5, 2014, and runs through December 31, 2015.

On a much smaller scale, the Chicago, Burlington & Quincy hired former FSA photographers Esther Bubley and Russell Lee to take pictures for its centennial history, *Granger Country: A Pictorial Social History of the Burlington Railroad* (1949). These images now are a part of the CB&Q archives at the Newberry Library which also houses records from the Illinois Central and Pullman Company.

Rail Enthusiast Photography

Chicago was a leader in commercial photography for railroads, but enthusiast photography evolved slowly. For Alfred W. Johnson (1896–1972), a commercial artist and

Alfred W. Johnson, a commercial artist and photographer, made color sketches on tracing paper to show his ideas for posters and calendars. The example here is of two C&NW passenger trains passing in the night. *John Gruber collection*

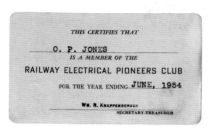

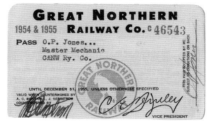

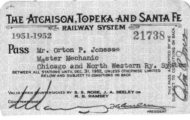

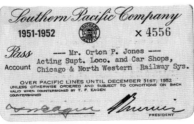

Orton Jones was a master mechanic on the Chicago & North Western based at Proviso for much of his career. Reciprocal agreements among the railroads allowed employees to secure travel passes such as these. *O. P. Jones collection*

illustrator, negatives date back to about 1918. He is well known for his imaginative views of passenger trains, coming and going. As might be expected, Johnson recorded the steam locomotive on the front of the train, but he also made many photos of the rear of the train. His work shows an artist's eye for creativity and details. Deeply interested in railroads around Chicago, he specialized in the Chicago & North Western but also roamed the Midwest. The C&NW distributed his painting of the 1939 streamlined *400*; colored tracings show his many other ideas for posters and calendars.

A friend, Francis Cole, started in photography at about the same time as Johnson. Others, inspired by the International Engine Picture Club founded in 1931 by *Railroad Stories* magazine, started trading photographs. Charlie Felstead (1917–1993) described his ideal locomotive photo. It was taken in good light at a 45-degree angle or lower and with no background. "We would purposely get them moved so there was as little as possible between us and the locomotive, and so at least the front was lighted," he said.

Enthusiast groups, beginning in the 1930s, encouraged photography. Among these were Railroad Club of Chicago, 1934, and Chicago Chapter of the Railway and Locomotive Historical Society (R&LHS), 1936, organized by thirteen charter members "who consider any locomotive engineer more glamorous than Gregory Peck," according to the *Chicago Tribune*. George Krambles, B. L. Stone, Frank E. Butts, A. C. Kalmbach, John F. Humiston, and Earl R. Thompson organized the Central Electric Railfans' Association in 1938. Women joined in—Verna Larsen, office manager for the Alfred O'Gara Company, was R&LHS secretary and editor of the chapter's publication. The Milwaukee Road and C&NW camera clubs encouraged employees to be creative in the late 1930s.

Only the guest is without a tie when members of the Chicago Chapter of the R&LHS, riding a Pennsylvania Railroad fan trip, line up at Fort Wayne, Indiana, on October 4, 1936: Mac Poor, MacKenzie, Charles Medin, Guthrie, Blair (guest), Repinske, Weiss, Harold Du Bal, Deffenbaugh, Finley, W. D. "Doc" Yungmeyer, Gillum, Allen, Osterholm, Alfred W. Johnson, Francis Cole, Wendell Ranke, and Ray Colombe. *Chicago Chapter Archives, R&LHS*

Books by Lucius Beebe (the first in 1938) encouraged railfan photography. When Beebe was in Chicago in 1939 to photograph the Rock Island Railroad for his second train book, a *Chicago Tribune* gossip columnist, June Provines, talked with him at a cocktail party. "There are as many rules governing the photographing of trains as there are about the classic French drama," she quoted him. He asserted that ideal photos should include country typical of the run and smoke trails to indicate motion. Provines concluded that Beebe failed to live up to his reputation for elegant grooming, including a diamond

gardenia brooch for his lapel. "It is only fair to add that the three times we saw Mr. Beebe he was drinking and not eating, the diamond gardenia was not in evidence, he had on the same brown suit, and once he needed a shave," she said.

In the foreword to that book, *Highliners: a Railroad Album* (1940), Beebe noted that not all photographs "abide by the most rigid classic requirements. Some have been taken from other than the three-quarters head-on angle required by exacting collectors of action shots."

In the 1940s, some South Side Chicago residents spent a lot of time together: Merle

Anderson, Sid Davies, Paul Eilenburger, Charlie Felstead, Milt Nafus, Jim Schmidt, and Delmar W. "Doc" Yungmeyer. Eilenburger was the baggageman at Englewood Union Station. You can see them on the website Ancient Chicago Area Railfans.

Paul E. Slager, Henry J. McCord, Phil Weibler, and others specialized in action views of the railroad and its surroundings. Slager, who said he had a "lust for travel and curiosity about everything," earned a bachelor's degree in business administration from Northwestern University. Slager started in Streator, where he graduated from high school in 1932, photographing employees standing in front of engines at the roundhouse and aerial views from Curtiss Jenny airplanes. He photographed the last steam engines out of Chicago, and then traveled to Europe thirteen times to record the last of steam in western European countries.

McCord, a self-taught mechanical engineer who lived in St. Charles, traveled across the Midwest making railroad photographs, especially of the Milwaukee Road. *Trains* featured a series he made in 1949 near his home of the Illinois Central where it crosses the Fox River. McCord, general manager of Reason Manufacturing in St. Charles, did portrait photography as a side business. His career ended tragically with his death in a traffic accident in 1957.

Weibler, who earned a bachelor of fine arts degree in industrial design at the University of Illinois, is a career railroader, working for the Norfolk & Western, 1956; Rock Island, 1960–1972; and Chicago & North Western, 1975–1999. While at Illinois, he often saw fellow fans such as Jim Boyd, J. Parker Lamb, and Bruce Meyer, with whom he made photo trips in 1958 and 1959. Weibler's coverage has ranged from such locations as the C&NW passenger terminal and Grand Central Station in Chicago to CB&Q in the Midwest and Chesapeake & Ohio in West Virginia. "The serpentine form of the train and the rails suggests motion. Look for work which goes beyond even 'panned' images to utilize techniques seen in music videos and in advertising. That should get folks excited," he advised.

Reflecting on this photo of a nun at Chicago Union Station, David P. Morgan, editor of *Trains*, wrote "It could be a cathedral." *John Gruber*

Union Station's photographic significance comes from two happenings: a photo story in *Trains* in 1965 and the first multimedia slide show in 1969. Initially, Kaufmann & Fabry, the large commercial photography company serving many of the railroads in the city, produced the publicity photos. As might be expected, Alfred W. Johnson recorded activity at the station along with passenger train views throughout the city. The FSA OWI photographers visited the station in World War II. But for a station of its scope, the photo selections are sparse.

Perhaps that's a reason David P. Morgan, then *Trains* editor, asked for photographs of the station in 1964. "Come with us now as John Gruber explores a structure grand enough to occupy an architect and a train-watcher," Morgan wrote in the introduction to the thirteen-page photo-essay published in the August 1965 issue.

Mel Patrick followed with a multimedia show with two projectors and music, previewed at Central Station and initially presented for the Railroad Club of Chicago. "Chicago Union Station-A Photographic Narrative" runs 23½ minutes. It is introduced with a short narration, then uses six songs to drive a segmented look at people and trains that use the station. Photos by Patrick and Larry Sallee were very carefully selected to accompany the music to produce a coherent match between sight and sound," said Patrick, a Chicago native. "The concept of using narration and music to accompany slides did not originate with me by any means, but this was the first full-scale attempt at a railroad-theme program with fast-paced dissolved images."

Mike Schafer, who was in the audience, continued the trend. Schafer is best known for "Silver Memory," about the *California Zephyr* (1970), and "Chicago Is … My Kind of Railroad Town" (1971). He has revamped and automated both shows, produced initially with Jim Heuer and others in the North Western Illinois Chapter-NRHS, Rockford. Patrick's innovative night exposures appeared in the *Illinois Central Magazine* in December 1968.

David Plowden, who lives in Winnetka, has for five decades documented America's vanishing landscapes and artifacts in stunning black-and-white photography. His exhibition, *Industrial Landscape of Chicago*, was at the Chicago History Museum in 1985. His more than twenty books include *Requiem for Steam: The Railroad Photographs of David Plowden* (2010) with 140 tritone photographs of the last of the steam locomotives.

The transition from film to digital cameras—peak years were 2003 to 2006—produced more change and an increasing emphasis on the Internet for sharing and showing photographs. The Internet allows instantaneous exchange of information about trains between trackside observers.

"For a self-taught photographer who had a lifetime of experience with film, the advent of digital imaging was neither welcome nor did I think helpful. I was wrong," Patrick said. "Two events sold me on digital. First, when making a slide presentation to a rail club luncheon, a digital projector was being used for some introductory information; I looked at the brightness of the digital projection, compared that to the slide projector and decided then I should scan my own slides for group presentation and as a side benefit I'd then be able to post images on the internet. A second revelation came when looking at one of Joe McMillan's new railroad calendars. He asked if I could identify which of the images was the first digital original he used. I could indeed spot the lone digital image; it was the only one not showing grain in the sky. I knew then that if I wanted the best possible image quality, digital would be the choice.

"My first experience with my own digital camera taught me the benefits of digital: instant feedback on image quality, no worrying about a pending 'end of roll,' digital storage of images, color balance in the camera, high ISO speeds, and an uncanny ability to capture images in very low light. I know of only one remaining advantage with film, the ability to hold color and detail in very bright light (sky, shooting into the sun or headlights). Despite this, there's no going back."

Posters and Commercial Art

The electric interurban railroads and utilities offered the twentieth century's best railroad poster campaign focusing on a single urban area in the United States. The companies were bold, innovative, and artistic in their pursuit of passengers and freight. The posters are among the most colorful—and taken for granted— examples of American commercial art.

The Chicago posters, influenced by the London Underground artwork, started appearing in 1922 on properties managed by English born industrialist Samuel Insull, who was assembling an empire of electric railways and utility companies. Britton I. Budd, who served as president of many of the Insull companies, was the person most directly responsible for the posters and other aggressive public relations activities to boost ridership.

"Chicago Elevated Vies with London Underground in Beauty of Traction Posters," the *Electric Traction Journal* proclaimed when it reproduced five examples from the North Shore Line and Chicago Rapid Transit. The posters stand out "markedly from the usual type of advertising which appears on the stations," the trade journal said.

A national magazine published in New York City praised Budd for initiating the series. "The Chicago railway officials saw the posters from the London Underground and French railways and decided to make their own billboards more attractive," according to the *World's Work*.

An experiment with the Field Museum showed how effective the posters were. The museum had not advertised before, but allowed the Chicago railroads to produce a design with a seahorse. In three weeks, museum attendance tripled, and museum officials complained when the poster came down.

Insull's companies produced about two hundred posters focusing on attractions in southern Wisconsin, northern Illinois, and northern Indiana. The posters taken as a whole show an entire urban region—admittedly idealized but still very comprehensive. They did a job that more likely would be handled by a regional chamber of commerce today.

Following their introduction in Chicago, main-line railroads and the Pullman Company created poster campaigns. Leslie Ragan (1897– 1972) did work both in Chicago and in New York City for the New York Central. Posters by William P. Welsh (1889–1984) for Pullman Company were more innovative than the company itself.

Commercial artists received business from the railroads. A host of calendar artists called Chicago home. Paul Proehl (1887–1965) is credited with artwork for at least eleven C&NW calendars between 1938 and 1952, also reproduced on such items as dining car menus, plus posters and illustrations for Illinois Central, CB&Q,

Ervine Metzel's poster for the North Shore Line won prizes early in his career. Later, from 1957 to 1960, Metzel designed ten postage stamps for the U.S. Postal Service. *J. J. Sedelmaier collection*

Albert W. Miller's *Man at Work* oil painting of a scene at the Milwaukee Road's Bensenville Yard was commissioned in 1968 by a printing company. It is described as "a corporate expressionist style." *The Eckhart G. Grohmann Collection, Milwaukee School of Engineering*

and A Century of Progress Exposition in 1933 and 1934. Robert W. Addison (1924–1988) produced calendars for the Milwaukee Road. Pat Rosado (1923–1987) illustrated calendars and ads for the road featuring Susie, a self-reliant young traveler.

Later, Albert W. Miller (1917–2009) produced a large oil painting of a scene at the Milwaukee Road's Bensenville Yard. It was commissioned in 1968 by a printing company, presented to the railroad in 1975, and donated in 2005 to the Milwaukee School of Engineering for its *Man at Work: The Eckhart G. Grohmann Collection.*

Railroad Influence Continues

With its status as the nation's railroad center firmly established and its visual legacy well documented, recognition of Chicago's railroad history is moving forward:

- The Center for Railroad Photography & Art, a nonprofit organization incorporated in Wisconsin, has located its archives at Lake Forest College in Illinois and presents an annual conference, Conversations about Photography, at the college.
- Illinois Railway Museum, founded in 1953 and now located at Union, has the largest equipment collection of any railroad museum in the United States.
- Fox River Valley Trolley Museum at South Elgin opened in 1966.
- Millennium Park at 201 East Randolph Street between Michigan Avenue and Columbus Avenue illustrates reuse of former railroad property. The park is built on a steel superstructure over Illinois Central's original Chicago railroad yard. Opened in 2004, the 24.5-acre facility combines architecture, monumental sculpture, and landscape design.

- A Chicago landmark, the Beverly/ Morgan Park Railroad Station District recognizes stations built between 1889 and 1945 at 91st, 95th, 99th, 107th, 111th, and 115th Streets along the Metra Rock Island Suburban Line. The six structures in this thematic district represent rare surviving examples of late nineteenth- and early twentieth-century commuter railroad stations. Annette E. McCrea (1858–1928), while working for the Rock Island, planned landscape designs for some of these station grounds.

- The Commission on Chicago Landmarks has set up a list of railroads and bridges that played a role in the development of Chicago as a transportation center: the Chicago & North Western North Branch bridge and powerhouse, Chicago & Western Indiana bridge, Milwaukee Road bridge No. Z-2, Cortland Street drawbridge, Dearborn Street Station, Garfield Boulevard L station and overpass, Illinois Central swing bridges 1 and 2, LaSalle Street cable car powerhouse, Lake Shore & Michigan Southern bridges, Michigan Avenue bridge and esplanade, Pennsylvania Railroad bridges, the St. Charles Air Line bridge, and Union Station.

- *Tragedy to Triumph*, a sculpture Naperville artist Paul Kuhn created to memorialize those who died in the disastrous 1946 crash in Naperville (see Chapter 2), is made entirely of recycled railroad parts. The sculpture was dedicated April 26, 2014, one day after the sixty-eighth anniversary of the crash.

- The Pullman State Historic Site honors Chicago railroad history and could become a national park. In 1991, the State of Illinois purchased the 12.66-acre Clock Tower and Administration Building. After nearly being destroyed by a fire in 1998, the state stabilized the North Factory and reconstructed the shell of the tower, but progress has been slow. The Hotel Florence, now a part of the site, is undergoing renovation.

A reconnaissance survey in 2013 by the National Park Service's Midwest Region explained the site's importance: "In addition to a broader understanding of Pullman in labor history, the district is potentially also significant for its role in the history of industry, commerce, and transportation history."

Two African American unions had headquarters on the south side of Chicago: the Brotherhood of Sleeping Car Porters and the Joint Council of Dining Car Employees. Cook County, which includes Chicago, had 8,212 railroad employees in 2011. **Below:** Leland C. Cain, a retired dining car chef and member of the Joint Council of Dining Car Employees (photographed at Madison, Wisconsin, in 1980), said: "The Cain family knows a good thing when they find it. My father was a railroader, I was a railroader, my son is a railroader, I had a daughter who was a railroader, and she was in the yards. Working for the railroad was the best thing that ever happened to my family." *Henry A. Koshollek*

CHAPTER 4

Contemporary Chicagoland Operations

By Chris Guss

Chicago remains America's largest railway hub and is a fascinating place to witness the movement of goods and people via its vast network of rail lines. The volume of rail traffic that passes through the city each day is staggering. Approximately 1,300 trains haul mixed freight, coal, intermodal, perishables, passengers, and so on. It remains one of the premier locations for east and west Class 1 railroads to interchange traffic. Canadian National and Canadian Pacific both entered the Chicago area via mergers and acquisitions giving Chicago the distinction of the only place where all Class 1s in the United States and Canada meet, with the exception of Kansas City Southern (though it serves Chicago through a haulage arrangement with CP).

Coverage in this chapter is focused on the trackage and operations inside the loop of Canadian National (former Elgin Joliet & Eastern) trackage from Waukegan on the north side of Chicago to Kirk Yard on the far southeast corner. Some trackage and facilities outside this area are detailed as necessary to clarify Chicago area workings. Not all lines or operations are covered; rather, this is an overview of operations of major corridors current as of fall/winter 2013.

Opposite page: A westward BNSF double stack snakes over the Chicago Sanitary and Ship Canal. (See page 154.) *Don Kalkman*

Above: Metra 105 eastbound catches the last light of the sun as it passes a Norfolk Southern local east of Tower A2 on Canadian Pacific's C&M Subdivision. NS still works the former Panhandle line as the successor to the Pennsylvania Railroad. The Panhandle's circuitous route and many at grade crossings with other railroads caused PRR to shift passenger trains onto its former Fort Wayne route south from Union Station in the 1930s. *Adam Pizante;* **Below:** With Lake Michigan on the horizon, Norfolk Southern business train 951 sails eastbound through CP 509 and over the Calumet River on the railroad's Chicago Line on September 9, 2013. In the background is South Chicago and Indiana Harbor Railway's yard. The train will leave Illinois and enter Indiana in less than a mile. *Chris Guss*

Passenger Operations

Amtrak

Chicago is Amtrak's primary Midwestern hub and is one of the most important nodes on Amtrak's national network. Chicago Union Station serves as the terminal for twenty-eight daily trains, running on six regional corridors and eight long-distance routes. Union Station is Amtrak's fourth-busiest station (after New York Penn Station, Philadelphia 30th Street, and Washington, D.C., Union Station), accommodating nearly 3.4 million Amtrak passengers in 2011.

Amtrak trains largely serve routes adapted from historical services provided by the railroads prior to 1971, but some of these routes had to be altered to reach Union Station (instead of their historic terminals) and also as result of abandonment and route consolidation following railroad mergers.

Amtrak's present long-distance routes evolved from its original basic system. Typically, long-distance trains carry sleeping cars and diners in addition to coaches. Corridor routes (under recent legislation) require state sponsorship, and they provide more frequent services than long-distance runs offer. Many corridor trains employ push-pull trainsets to simplify operations, obviating the need to turn trains or run around locomotives at outlying terminals. Where long-distance trains reach to the coasts, corridor runs radiate from Chicago to cities within a 320-mile radius.

Michigan Corridor trains serve three separate eastern terminals: *Pere Marquette* (train 370/371) to Grand Rapids, *Blue Water* to Port Huron, and *Wolverine Service* to Detroit and Pontiac. The Indiana Corridor consists only of four trains to Indianapolis per week, the *Hoosier State* (trains 850/851) that

fills alternate days missed by the triweekly long-distance *Cardinal*. Both *Hoosier State* and *Cardinal* use Metra's Southwest Corridor (mostly the Chicago & Western Indiana) between Union Station and 81st Street, then Union Pacific's Villa Grove Subdivision (former C&EI) from 81st Street to Thornton, and CSXT's Elsdon Subdivision (former CN, née GTW) to Munster to reach CSX's Monon Subdivision. In addition to its role as a passenger train, the *Hoosier State* shuttles equipment to and from Amtrak's former New York Central Beech Grove shops near Indianapolis.

Southern Illinois services to Carbondale consist of the daily *Saluki* (trains 390/391) and *Illini* (392/393), which run via Canadian National's Chicago Subdivision (former Illinois Central) from Union Station. To reach CN's former IC main line, these trains use the St. Charles Air Line from Union Interlocking at the south end of Amtrak's Union Station facilities.

An inbound Metra Electric train departs the Roosevelt Road Station headed for Van Buren Street Station on April 20, 2007. *Craig Williams*

Chicago–St. Louis trains, dubbed *Lincoln Service* (trains 300/301, 302/303, 304/305, and 306/307), run via the former Alton/Gulf Mobile & Ohio route (now Canadian National's Joliet Subdivision between 21st Street and Joliet, and beyond Joliet Union Pacific's Joliet Subdivision). Corridor trains to Quincy, Illinois, are provided by *Illinois Zephyr* (380/383) and *Carl Sandburg* (381/382), which use BNSF's historic Chicago, Burlington & Quincy routing.

Amtrak's busiest Chicago-area service is the Chicago–Milwaukee *Hiawatha* route on the historic Milwaukee Road, with seven roundtrips daily and six on Sunday (trains 331/332, 333/334, 335/336, 337/338, 339/340, 341/342; and 329/330 Monday–Saturday). This route carried nearly eighty thousand passengers a month in 2013. Trains leave from the north side of Union Station on Metra's Milwaukee North line and Canadian Pacific's C&M Subdivision. Today's *Hiawathas* are limited to 79 miles per hour, making the run in one hour and twenty-nine minutes.

Although Chicago benefits from more long-distance routes than any other Midwestern city, these eight routes are a far cry from the level of service during the passenger train's golden age. Daily East Coast trains are the *Capitol Limited* (29/30) to Washington, D.C., via Pittsburgh and the *Lake Shore Limited* (48-448/49-449) between Chicago and New York/Boston. Both use Norfolk Southern's Chicago Line (former Lake Shore & Michigan Southern/NYC) on the Chicago leg of their journeys. In addition, the triweekly *Cardinal* to Washington (50/51) runs via Indianapolis and Cincinnati.

Amtrak's *City of New Orleans* (58/59) runs to its namesake south from Union Station

Metra and Amtrak trains pass in the evening at Roosevelt Road on the approach to Union Station. This bridge spanning many tracks has been a popular vantage point for railroad photographers for decades. To the east of the main lines are Amtrak's 12th Street car shops. *Don Kalkman*

along the same former Illinois Central route as the Southern Illinois Corridor trains. The *Texas Eagle* (21/22) runs to San Antonio, Texas, via the former Alton/GM&O to St. Louis.

Amtrak's *Southwest Chief* (3/4) to Los Angeles and *California Zephyr* (5/6) to California's Bay Area use BNSF's former Burlington lines via Aurora to Galesburg, Illinois, where their routes diverge. Historically, Great Northern's *Empire Builder* to Seattle and Portland used a Burlington routing, but today's train (7/8) runs via CP's former Milwaukee Road Hiawatha Corridor to Milwaukee and beyond to the Twin Cities where it joins BNSF's route to the Pacific Northwest.

Amtrak's Chicago-area operations include five regional dispatcher desks based in Union Station, plus its 14th Street car shops and 16th Street diesel shops, located south of Union Station. Additional maintenance is performed by Amtrak's Brighton Park car shop (situated along Canadian National's former Alton, now Joliet Subdivision).

Unlike push-pull corridor trainsets, Amtrak's long-distance trains are unidirectional and thus require turning upon arrival in Chicago. Most trainsets are dedicated to one specific service, but the *City of New Orleans* and *Texas Eagle* are exceptions that share trainsets in order to simplify Chicago terminal operations. Because the *City of New Orleans* uses the St. Charles Air Line and must make a reverse move into and out of Union Station, Amtrak sends the train set out as the *Texas Eagle*, thus saving a turning move. Likewise, the inbound *Texas Eagle* becomes the outbound *City of New Orleans*.

Metra

Metra is the commuter rail division of Chicago area's Regional Transportation Authority. It operates over seven hundred weekday commuter trains on 487 route-miles in eleven corridors radiating from downtown Chicago.

As a function of historical precedents, Metra trains still serve four distinct downtown terminals, including Union Station, which is shared with Amtrak. Except for former Illinois Central electrified lines operated as Metra

Amtrak train 383, the *Illinois Zephyr*, sails above traffic in downtown Aurora as it races west on BNSF's Chicago Subdivision with passengers traveling from Chicago to Quincy, Illinois. The former CB&Q main line is elevated through the heart of the city from just west of Eola Yard to the Aurora control point on the west side of town where the Chicago Subdivision ends and the Aurora and Mendota Subdivisions begin. Leading the train is Amtrak General Electric-built P42 No. 42 specially painted to honor American veterans. Entering service in November 1971, the *Illinois Zephyr* was Amtrak's first state-supported train. *Sayre Kos*

Electric, all Metra passenger services are push-pull diesel-powered gallery-style trains with locomotives facing outbound.

Union Station serves the largest number of lines with trains working both north and south from this central hub: former Milwaukee Road routes Milwaukee North (to Fox Lake) and Milwaukee West (to Elgin); BNSF Railway's route to Aurora (former Burlington triple-track raceway); the Heritage Corridor to Joliet

(former Alton/GM&O route); Southwest Service to Orland Park and Manhattan (former Wabash/Norfolk & Western route); and since 1996, North Central Service to Antioch, via Canadian National north of Franklin Park (former Wisconsin Central/Soo Line route).

Oglivie Transportation Center (formerly North Western Station) is the terminal for the former C&NW routes, now operated by Union Pacific as the North, Northwest, and West services. LaSalle Street Station serves the former Rock Island suburban routes to Joliet via Blue Island, known as the Rock Island District. Millennium Station, formerly IC's Randolph Street, is the terminal for Metra Electric trains to University Park, plus branches to Blue Island and South Chicago, and also hosts South Shore electric trains to South Bend, Indiana, which use trackage rights via the Metra Electric District from Kensington to Millennium.

Above: A northbound Metra Electric train off the South Chicago Sub District prepares to enter the University Park Sub District at the 67th Street interlocking. In this view from the closed 67th Street station platform looking south, the double-track branch descends and passes under the trackage to the left of the train as it winds its way southeast five miles to the end of the line in South Chicago. *Chris Guss;* **Below:** With Chicago's Willis Tower dominating the skyline on November 30, 2011, all's quiet for the moment on the former Illinois Central south of the city. Here, four electrified main tracks of Metra's University Park Sub District parallel Canadian National's Chicago Subdivision located on the right of the photo. With over two hundred revenue passenger trains (including South Shore) daily on the electrified trackage and a half dozen Amtraks on Canadian National, plus the occasional freight, things won't stay quiet for long. *Craig Williams*

Staging and storage of Metra trains off peak, plus running maintenance and light repairs for its diesel-powered train-sets, is performed at various locations. Metra's Western Avenue facility (located north of Tower A2, where former C&NW routes from Oglivie Transportation Central cross former Milwaukee Road routes from Union Station) serves trains for the Heritage Corridor, Milwaukee District North, Milwaukee District West, and North Central routes. BNSF 14th Street shops downtown near Union Station maintains BNSF trains for the Aurora route as well as those assigned to Southwest Service. Heavy maintenance for all lines, including Rock Island District trains, is performed at the 47th Street shops in a facility still known as the Rocket House, a carryover from Rock Island's famous streamliners. KYD Yard (south of Kensington) is the primary Metra Electric heavy maintenance shop, with light maintenance handled at 18th Street Yard (near downtown). Wheel work is performed at the old Rock Island diesel shops at Burr Oak Yard in Blue Island, which also performs occasional contract work for other area railroads.

Above: Intricate trackage characteristic of Chicago's busy operations is displayed at the throat of Ogilvie Transportation Center (originally North Western Station). This web of trackage sorts 194 scheduled Metra trains plus dozens of light power and empty deadhead equipment moves serving the station daily. *John Ryan;* **Below:** BNSF SW1200 No. 3533 switches out the 14th Street shops just south of Union Station on January 4, 2008. Operated under a purchase of service agreement between BNSF and Metra, the railroad provides its own power to switch the yard and keep the trainsets ready to go when needed. *Sayre Kos*

On September 17, 2009, a rush-hour Metra train disgorges its passengers at the Elmhurst station on Union Pacific's Geneva Subdivision. All of Metra's trains are bi-directional, consisting of either push-pull sets with diesel locomotives and cab-control cars or multiple unit cars on the Metra Electric. *Pete Ruesch*

Although Metra is the umbrella organization for all Chicago-area commuter operations, the particulars of track ownership, dispatching, and equipment ownership vary from route to route as a result of historical arrangement with the railroads. Since 1982, many of Chicago's commuter corridors have been purchased and are operated directly by Metra. However, there are two primary exceptions. On the former C&NW and Burlington routes, Union Pacific and BNSF Railway operate Metra trains under purchase of service agreements, whereby the maintenance of cars and engines, plus train crews and tracks needed to operate

the trains, are supplied by those respective railroads. The Southwest Service route is leased from Norfolk Southern, which continues to dispatch the line, while Heritage Corridor trains use Canadian National's Joliet Subdivision, and North Central Service uses Canadian Pacific's Elgin Sub between Union Station and Tower B12 (Franklin Park) and then Canadian National's Waukesha Sub to Antioch.

Metra's train dispatchers are located in offices immediately south of BNSF's 14th Street shops. Weekdays, eight dispatcher desks oversee operations. These are combined into four desks on nights and weekends.

Above: Northern Indiana Commuter Transportation District's newest cars for the South Shore Line Chicago–South Bend, Indiana, service are gallery-style bi-level electric multiple units built by Nippon-Sharyo in 2008–2009. A set of the new cars are seen at Hammond, Indiana, approaching State Line Interlocking on September 28, 2010. *Pete Ruesch*; **Below:** Northern Indiana Commuter Transportation District's South Shore trains terminate in Metra's downtown Millennium Station (formerly Illinois Central's Randolph Street terminal). These single-level stainless steel electric cars were custom-built by Nippon-Sharyo in 1982–1983 to replace ancient interurban electric cars built by Pullman and Pressed Steel in the mid-1920s. *Ray Weart*

South Shore

The Northern Indiana Commuter Transportation District is today's operator of the historic South Shore, overhead-electric, interurban line that runs from South Bend, Indiana, to downtown Chicago. It provides a suburban-style passenger service while also hosting freight traffic provided by a separate company. (See Chapter 1.)

The railroad enters the Chicago area at Gary, Indiana. To reach Chicago's downtown Millennium Station, South Shore commuter trains connect with Metra's Electric District at Kensington Tower. Weekdays, South Shore operates eighteen westbound and nineteen eastbound trains into Chicago, with half that number on weekends.

Dwindling Towers

Hundreds of towers once controlled the trackage that crisscrossed the Chicago area. Over the years, automation has taken its toll on manned towers. Only sixteen towers remained at beginning of the CREATE project (see Chapter 1), which further identified twelve towers for closure with their functions transferred to remote locations. As of late 2013, seven of these have closed: 21st Street, Blue Island, Calumet Tower, Gresham, Kensington, Hick, and Deval. In 2013, Metra was installing equipment to close Canadian Pacific's former Milwaukee Road towers B-17 (on the Elgin Subdivision) and A-5 (at Pacific Junction on the C&M Subdivision). The remaining three towers to be closed by CREATE improvements are Rondout Tower on Canadian Pacific's C&M Subdivision, 16th Street Tower on Metra's Joliet Sub District (south of La Salle Street Station), and Metra's Blue Island tower on the Blue Island Sub District.

A Norfolk Southern DASH9-40CW blasts past Hick Tower at CP503 on NS's Chicago Line at East Chicago, Indiana. The tower controlled drawbridges over an artificial waterway that drains into Lake Michigan. Historically, Baltimore & Ohio, New York Central's Lake Shore & Michigan Southern, and Pennsylvania's Fort Wayne lines ran adjacent to each other here. The tower has since closed as a function of the CREATE project. *Mark Llanuza*

Tower A2, where Union Pacific's Geneva Subdivision (former C&NW) crosses Canadian Pacific's C&M Subdivision (former Milwaukee Road), is always busy. On October 23, 2008, eastbound Amtrak *Hiawatha* train 332 crosses over UP for its final sprint into Union Station. A Union Pacific train waits for the lineup into the California Avenue Coach Yard as a light engine heads around the corner and waits to enter Metra's Western Avenue Coach Yard. *Marshall W. Beecher*

An Amtrak *Hiawatha* bound for Milwaukee passes A2 tower, located two miles from Union Station. This exceptionally busy junction will retain its tower, despite operational improvements from Chicago's CREATE Project. This is a rare surviving example of a Union Switch & Signal Model 14 electro-pneumatic interlocking. Air-powered switch points are faster than electric switch machines. *Marshall W. Beecher*

Three towers are expected to remain open in the Chicago area outside the CREATE project changes: Joliet (UD) Tower (where BNSF's Chillicothe Sub and Union Pacific's Joliet Sub cross Metra's Joliet Sub District at grade, though this may be closed in connection with a new station at Joliet); Canadian National's West Chicago (JB) tower (where CN's Leithton Subdivision, the former EJ&E main line, crosses Union Pacific's Geneva Subdivision); and Metra's Tower A-2 on Canadian Pacific's C&M Subdivision.

Class 1 Freight Operations

America's largest freight railroads are the massive Class 1 carriers, each with thousands of route-miles. Although mergers have changed all the names, Chicago remains North America's largest single gateway; here all major players interchange, terminate, and originate traffic. All the major systems converge on Chicago: BNSF Railway, Canadian National, Canadian Pacific, CSXT, Norfolk Southern, and Union Pacific. These lines handle the majority of freight in the

region, using well-maintained routes inherited from predecessor companies.

At any one time, dozens of long freights are on the move in Chicago. In addition to the traditional carload manifest freights operating between major classification yards, modern point-to-point unit trains carry bulk commodities such as coal, crude oil, ethanol, and grain, plus intermodal container trains (commonly using double-stack cars), and automotive trains (carrying new cars and trucks from manufacturing plants to regional distribution centers).

BNSF

BNSF's primary Chicago routes are its former Santa Fe Chillicothe Subdivision and the former Chicago Burlington & Quincy/ Burlington Northern route.

The Chillicothe Sub reaching the Chicago area via Joliet is one of the premier freight main lines serving the area. This is the east end of Santa Fe's route between Chicago, Texas,

Above: A Canadian Pacific train and a Union Pacific transfer depart simultaneously eastbound from Bensenville Yard on October 30, 2013. The transfer will swing south on the Indiana Harbor Belt for the short trip to Proviso Yard while the CP train will head east to the Belt Railway of Chicago at Cragin. *Don Kalkman;* **Below:** A westward BNSF double stack snakes across the former Santa Fe double-track truss lift span over the Chicago Sanitary and Ship Canal at Lemont on the Chillicothe Subdivision. This line is the eastern end of BNSF's Chicago–California route, which has been one of America's premier intermodal corridors since Santa Fe times. *Don Kalkman*

In the spirit of Burlington Northern's 1970s-era hot piggyback train named the *Pacific Zip*, BNSF's ZCHCSSE7-09 (Chicago–South Seattle intermodal) roars west at Western Springs, Illinois, on November 9, 2013. Today railroaders know this busy three-track line as BNSF's Chicago Subdivision, yet many enthusiasts still descriptively call it the Triple Track, while railroaders know it as the East End. Movements on all three main tracks are authorized by centralized traffic control with bi-directional signaling, which allows dispatchers great flexibility. *Chris Guss*

and California. Unlike other busy freight routes, it isn't encumbered by passenger or commuter trains, leaving the line free to move transcontinental intermodal business, along with a mix of carload and automotive traffic. Intermodal trains are interchanged with CSX and Norfolk Southern via connections east of Corwith Yard at the Ash Street or Panhandle crossing. Union Pacific exercises trackage rights over the Chillicothe Subdivision (a function of the BN-Santa Fe merger granting SP rights in 1995, and UP's acquisition of SP in 1996), limited to intermodal and automotive traffic.

BNSF's former BN triple-track Chicago Subdivision main line, informally known as the Triple Track, runs west from Union Station and divides just west of Aurora. BNSF's Mendota Subdivision continues to Galesburg, Illinois, while its Aurora Subdivision (the C&I route described in Chapter 1) runs to Savanna with

connections beyond to the Twin Cities and Pacific Northwest. The triple-track Aurora to Chicago Union Station route is by far BNSF's busiest in the Chicago area. On a typical sample weekday in the fall of 2013, this route handled 163 scheduled trains: 61 BNSF freights, 8 Amtraks, and 94 Metra trains.

YARDS AND OPERATIONS

BNSF yards in the Chicago area are focused on specific traffic. Cicero Yard (at milepost 7 on the Chicago Subdivision) handles Chicago–Pacific Northwest intermodal traffic (running via former BN routes). Western Avenue Yard (east of Cicero at mile 3.7) serves as the interchange point for BNSF-NS run-through trains. Recently this has become busier as result of increased crude oil traffic moving east from North Dakota to points on Norfolk Southern for refining.

Most of BNSF's intermodal traffic is handled at three terminals located along the Chillicothe Subdivision (former Santa Fe main line). Corwith (six miles southwest of downtown) served as Santa Fe's primary yard prior to the BNSF merger, and at one time featured a hump yard to classify carload traffic. Corwith is now primarily a terminal for domestic container traffic. To the west, Willow Springs opened in 1994 concurrently with an adjacent United Parcel Service (UPS) sorting facility. (UPS has been an important Santa Fe/BNSF intermodal shipper.) Originally Willow Springs concentrated on trailer on flatcar (TOFC) piggyback shipments. However, in recent years the balance of its traffic has changed as UPS shifts gradually from TOFC to containers. BNSF's primary international container facility is located about ten miles west of Joliet and is called Logistics Park Chicago (despite its distance from the city). This modern facility opened in 2002 and also handles automotive traffic.

In addition to work performed at Chicago yards, eastward intermodal traffic destined for direct interchange with CSXT or NS is presorted at Fort Madison, Iowa. Some BNSF trains carrying Pacific Northwest international traffic that traditionally would have been routed via the Chicago Subdivision to Cicero instead reach Logistics Park Chicago via a dogleg move over Canadian National's former EJ&E route from Eola to Joliet to reach the Chillicothe Subdivision.

Where historically BNSF's predecessors classified carload freight to and from eastern connections at major Chicago yards (BN at Cicero and Santa Fe at Corwith), in 2013 BNSF's Chicago interchange carload traffic is classified at distant yards, including Galesburg, Illinois, and Northtown in Minneapolis. Through traffic is moved on run-through manifest trains with NS and CSXT running via Chicago interchanges.

BNSF's remaining Chicago-area carload yards at Eola, Willow Springs, Congress Park, and Joliet are largely used for handling traffic to local customers. Eola is at mile 33.4 on the Chicago Sub. It handles interchange traffic between BNSF and CN, as well as block swapping between manifest freights. In addition to local freights, Eola yard originates one manifest freight for Kansas City and a road switcher for Savanna. To facilitate the traffic increase via Canadian National's former EJ&E route, there are future plans to upgrade connections between BNSF, CN, and other eastern carriers. Frequently, BNSF must park loaded coal trains on the Mendota Subdivision, which limits line capacity. To overcome this, five new staging tracks at Eola for unit trains are planned.

Some of BNSF's Chicago-area manifest trains originate or terminate at either Belt Railway of Chicago's Clearing Yard, Indiana Harbor Belt's Blue Island Yard, or points east of Chicago on CN. IHB's Gibson Yard makes up automotive trains for BNSF.

Canadian National

Historically, Grand Trunk Western was CN's only presence in the Chicago area, accessed from Michigan. After failing to capture the Milwaukee Road in the 1980s, CN negotiated

Canadian National Train M394 departs downtown on the Chicago Subdivision. On the left is the adjacent four-main-track Metra Electric District, while Lake Shore Drive and Lake Michigan are to the east just beyond the trees. Both CN's and Metra's lines were historically owned and operated by Illinois Central. *Ryan Schoenfeldt*

haulage rights between Duluth–Superior and Chicago (first via BN, and later via Wisconsin Central). Since 1999, CN has aggressively expanded its Chicago-area operations, beginning with its acquisition of Illinois Central. Since that time, CN has accumulated six major terminal facilities in Chicago along several different routes. CN went from having one of the simplest Chicago terminal operations to one of the most complicated as mergers with Wisconsin Central and Elgin, Joliet & Eastern resulted in traffic handling changes. Specifically, CN's integration of EJ&E has allowed it to route trains entirely around Chicago over its own lines—making it the only major railroad in the area with such flexibility. On the downside, EJ&E's numerous grade-level crossings of other railroads, several with intensive Metra services, can make running times across the route unpredictable.

KIRK YARD

Kirk Yard was EJ&E's primary terminal, strategically located adjacent to its primary customer, U.S. Steel's Gary Works. (EJ&E was owned by USS for many years.) Historically, Kirk classified thousands of cars from the steel works and other nearby heavy industries. Originally Kirk was a flat switching yard, but massive re-construction between 1950-52 transformed it into a hump yard with a 58-track bowl featuring an early automatic retarder control and automatic switch installations. Declines in the American steel industry resulted in considerable loss of traffic at Kirk. However, CN's acquisition of EJ&E has brought about the yard's rejuvenation. Since 2009, CN has developed Kirk as its primary Chicago-area freight classification facility, including an eight-track north receiving/departure yard, a 10-track south receiving/departure yard, and a single track hump yard with a 52-track classification bowl.

In 2013, Kirk originated four and terminated five manifest freight trains daily operating to various points on the CN network. Kirk originates one of CN's long-distance manifest train schedules forwarding empty forest product cars to northern British Columbia, 2,150 miles

Elgin, Joliet & Eastern was known as the Chicago Outer Belt and operated a 130-mile ring running from Porter, Indiana, to Waukegan, Illinois, with branches to South Chicago, Coal City (cut back to Goose Lake in the 1930s), and Aurora, Illinois. After working the interchange with Canadian Pacific at Rondout, Illinois, this J crew is turning the power on the connection before heading back to Joliet. This view was made from the old North Shore's Libertyville branch right of way. EJ&E's stations were measured from Joliet; with Rondout being mile 65.5. *Sayre Kos*

away. Since 2010, Kirk has terminated an NS run-through train operating over CN's GTW route from South Bend, Indiana. Because Kirk is adjacent to NS and CSX main lines, it is well suited as an interchange point. The yard continues to serve U.S. Steel, accommodating both carload traffic and unit coal and coke trains (from NS and CSX).

CN'S CHICAGO INTERMODAL TERMINALS

Markham Yard was Illinois Central's largest and most active Chicago-area yard. Historically, this was an important hump yard classifying traffic on IC's Chicago–New Orleans main line. Prior to CN's acquisition, IC routed significant interchange traffic between Markham and CN's Grand Trunk Western since the GTW main line crosses under the IC main line at the extreme north end of the yard. Before CN bought IC, there was considerable cooperation between the roads. In the 1990s, IC eliminated the hump and classification bowl tracks to make room for an intermodal facility, jointly operated with CN. This allowed CN to develop its eastern Canada–Chicago intermodal business, facilitated by the new-in-1995 St. Clair River tunnel between Michigan and Ontario, which clears double-stack containers. After it closed Markham's hump, IC accommodated some switching in surviving yard tracks while shifting remaining work to its Glenn Yard.

On November 11, 2013, a pair of Canadian National SD70M-2s bring intermodal train Q14921-09 into the Chicago Intermodal Terminal at Markham Yard. This train originates at CN's Montreal Intermodal Terminal and arrives in the Chicago area over former Grand Trunk Western trackage to Griffith, then the former EJ&E to Matteson before turning north on the former Illinois Central to Markham. *Pat Yough*

Canadian National's former Illinois Central Woodcrest Shops at Homewood, Illinois, remain an active locomotive servicing and repair facility. This view shows former Wisconsin Central GP40s being serviced prior to leaving the property. *Craig Williams*

After CN's acquisition of IC, Markham Yard continued to handle a substantial amount of general freight business. However, since the acquisition of EJ&E, most freight classification has moved to Kirk. This allowed continued expansion of Markham's intermodal footprint, making room for new warehousing and trans loading facilities and expansion of automobile unloading ramps. In 2013, Markham's Chicago Intermodal Terminal (CIT) originated and terminated at least four train pairs daily. Among other changes, CN's new ocean container port at Prince Rupert, British Columbia, now has direct service to Chicago.

JOLIET

Historically, EJ&E's Joliet Yard served as a gathering point for traffic on the western end of the railroad. Except for unit coal and ore trains, plus trackage rights trains using the line between UP/BNSF and the CN connection at Griffith, all of EJ&E's road freights originated or terminated at Joliet. At the time of CN's

acquisition, Joliet yard had seventy-five tracks with capacity for approximately 2,300 cars. However, CN has completely transformed operations at Joliet. It has shifted most of its through trains transiting Chicago to the EJ&E line between Matteson and Leithton. As a result, Joliet became an important crew change point for manifest freights, and effectively replaced crew changes at Schiller Park, Glenn Yard, and Markham Yard. CN also redeveloped part of the facility into a small intermodal terminal, which opened in summer 2013 to accommodate western Canada container traffic.

Joliet continues to serve as a hub for local freight, with five daily trains serving locations as far as the CP interchange at Spaulding, and an industrial area on CN's Illinois River Subdivision near Morris. Joliet is also an interchange point for unit trains (oil and coal from BNSF and UP, and empty autorack moves) and a daily pair of manifest trains operated with BNSF between southern Ontario and Galesburg.

CN'S GLENN, HAWTHORNE, AND SCHILLER PARK YARDS

CN's Glenn Yard had been the primary Chicago yard for Gulf, Mobile & Ohio. Although not on any major CN freight corridor, its strategic location near Ingredion's Argo (Corn Products) plant keeps its nineteen-track classification yard active. Here local traffic is accommodated, including transfer runs to Markham or Kirk Yards and BRC's nearby Clearing Yard, although as of 2014 no through freights called at the yard.

Hawthorne, with thirteen sorting tracks, plus storage and repair tracks, is a former IC yard along the Iowa main line. It handles local traffic, trains between Iowa lines and BRC, and interchange trains from NS's Calumet Yard. Unit ethanol trains from Iowa to Chicago interchange points change crews here.

CN inherited Schiller Park yard facilities with the acquisition of Wisconsin Central Limited in 2001. Initially Schiller was an important CN crew change for trains using the WC route, as well as a staging yard for traffic moving through Chicago via IHB, CP/BRC, or B&OCT routes to IC and GTW terminals on Chicago's South Side. However, since CN's diversion of most through traffic via the former EJ&E, the role of Schiller Park has been drastically scaled back. As of 2013, it serves primarily as a staging area for trains operating between western Canada or Wisconsin and BRC's Clearing Yard, and as a home terminal for a daily road switcher.

Canadian Pacific

Canadian Pacific operates three main routes into the Chicago area: two former Milwaukee Road lines, the C&M Sub running north toward Milwaukee and beyond to the Twin Cities, and the Elgin Sub running west to Savanna, Illinois. The third route is CP's trackage rights on Norfolk Southern east to Detroit, Michigan, where traffic continues into Canada on CP's own lines.

On December 13, 2010, Canadian Pacific Train 721 (running as Norfolk Southern symbol 33T) swings off the NS Chicago Line via control point 502 (CP502) onto NS-owned, Indiana Harbor Belt–operated trackage in East Chicago, Indiana. (A control point is a remote-controlled interlocking.) Train 721 operates between Toronto and Canadian Pacific's Bensenville Yard and carries autoracks to IHB's Gibson Yard. The train is threading though the ArcelorMittal Indiana Harbor steel plant; the lead locomotive is crossing the site of the former IHB/Pennsylvania Railroad diamonds. The former Fort Wayne line has been removed between Tolleston and control point 506 (CP506). *Chris Guss*

A Canadian Pacific empty ethanol train rolls west on Main Two past Galewood Yard and Metra's Hanson Park Station on Canadian Pacific's Elgin Subdivision. The train has just exited the Belt Railway main line at Cicero West (Cragin) and is headed back to the rural Midwest for reloading. *Marshall W. Beecher*

The C&M Subdivision, owned by Metra, is CP's busiest Chicago-area route. Its thirty-two miles between Chicago and Rondout host a mix of Amtrak, Metra, and Wisconsin & Southern (WSOR), as well as CP's own traffic. There are several key junctions northward from Union Station.

Tower A-2 (approximately two miles from Union Station) is CP's crossing of Union Pacific's Geneva Subdivision (former C&NW). Tower A-5 (Pacific Junction) is the connection between the Elgin (former Chicago & Pacific) and C&M Subdivisions. To accommodate the large volume of Metra suburban trains, the C&M route is equipped with three main tracks between Union Station and A5, and two main tracks beyond. The C&M from Union Station to A20 is primarily a passenger line with occasional freights running via A5 to access the east end of Bensenville Yard. The junction at Tower A20 (roughly twenty miles from Union Station) is CP's connection with Union Pacific's Milwaukee Subdivision, used by the majority of CP freights to Bensenville (running via Shermer and Bryn Mawr, and CP's Elgin Subdivision at Tower B17).

At Rondout, where the seventeen-mile Fox Lake Subdivision diverges, CP crosses Canadian National's Waukegan Subdivision between Leithton and Waukegan. This line is used by Metra's Milwaukee North trains (to Fox Lake, Illinois), and nightly Wisconsin & Southern freights between BRC's Clearing Yard and Janesville, Wisconsin.

West from Tower A5, CP's Elgin Subdivision runs thirty-five miles to its namesake, with Metra ownership extending beyond to Pingree Grove. Spaulding is the junction with CN's Leithton Subdivision (the former EJ&E) where CP interchanges with CN. A local from Bensenville makes regular turns to Spaulding for interchange traffic.

Canadian Pacific's Chicago–Detroit route is composed entirely of trackage rights on other railroads. Traffic from Bensenville travels via the BRC between Cragin (at milepost 2.3 on the CP's Elgin Subdivision) and control point 509 (CP509), where it joins Norfolk Southern's Chicago Line (at 95th Street just west of the Illinois-Indiana state line). CP's automotive traffic uses Indiana Harbor Belt's Gibson Yard (reached by diverging from NS's Chicago Line at control point 502 [CP502]).

CP YARDS AND OPERATIONS

Bensenville Yard, Canadian Pacific's sprawling former Milwaukee Road terminal located at

On October 21, 2007, southward CSX manifest Q649 crosses double-track EJ&E diamonds at Jay Tower, Chicago Heights, Illinois. This interlocking is located at milepost 27 on Union Pacific's Villa Grove Subdivision (shared with CSX). Both UP and CSX trains use this former Chicago & Eastern Illinois route, but UP handles dispatching. *Eric Powell*

milepost 15.5 along the Elgin Sub, handles most of CP's Chicago freight, with some traffic classified at BRC's Clearing Yard. The Bensenville hump was closed in early 2013 as part of a systemwide restructuring. The Bensenville intermodal facility stretches along the south side of the yard, handling only containers.

CP operates approximately twenty trains daily in and out of Chicago. Most are manifest carload trains, although some carry a mix of carload, automotive, or intermodal traffic. Bensenville has five pairs of daily manifest trains: two east, two north, and one west. Four dedicated intermodal services connect Chicago with Montreal, Quebec, and Vancouver, British Columbia. In addition, crude oil and ethanol trains are common.

Galewood Yard (seven miles east of Bensenville at milepost 8.7) sees CP unit trains for interchange with eastern lines (via BRC).

In addition, Galewood accommodates Indiana Rail Road (INRD) unit coke trains (run via CP trackage rights, see below).

CSX Transportation

The Chicago Division of CSX Transportation (CSX) is based in Calumet City, Illinois. Along with divisional management offices, this office has five CSX dispatcher desks plus two Indiana Harbor Belt dispatchers. CSX's Elsdon, Barr, Lake, Porter, Woodland, and Chicago Heights Subdivisions are handled by what's called the RA desk. The RB desk manages the Altenheim, Blue Island, Monon, and New Rock Subdivisions. RL dispatches the Lincoln, Pemberville, and Toledo Terminal Subdivisions. RN handles Detroit, Fremont, Grand Rapids, Grand Rapids Terminal, Plymouth, Port Huron, and Saginaw Subdivisions. RM is responsible for the Garrett Subdivision.

CSX Chicago operations involve two major corridors and three secondary routes. Most CSX traffic runs over the former Baltimore and Ohio east-west main line (now operated as the Barr Subdivision) and the former C&EI route jointly operated with Union Pacific as its Villa Grove Subdivision (sixty-six miles between Dolton and Woodland Junction). CSX's Monon Subdivision is a vestige of the former Monon's Chicago main line, running from Munster southward (via a connection off Canadian National's South Bend Subdivision), exiting the Chicago area after crossing Canadian National's Matteson Subdivision (ex-EJ&E) at Dyer, Indiana. A vestige of the Michigan Central is the Porter Subdivision from Indiana Harbor Belt's Gibson Yard toward Willow Creek. In addition to CSX's own freight, this line accommodates Norfolk Southern trains running from Porter Junction to NS's Kankakee Line south of Gibson.

Part of CSX's Chicago-area operations, unrelated to its historic predecessors, is the New Rock Subdivision, which takes its name from the former Rock Island main, a portion of which CSX acquired after Rock was liquidated. This runs west from Joliet to Ottawa and Bureau. (Rock's Bureau–Peoria line is now operated by Iowa Interstate.) CSX New Rock freights reach Joliet via Metra's Joliet Sub District from Blue Island (also former Rock Island).

In the Chicago terminal, trackage is owned by CSX subsidiary Baltimore & Ohio Chicago Terminal. The Blue Island Subdivision extends from Vermont Street near its namesake to a connection with Union Pacific north of Ash Street at Ogden Junction. The Barr Subdivision begins at Vermont Street and continues eastward through Barr Yard to Dolton, State Line Interlocking, and Clarke Junction.

CSX operates three primary terminals, in addition to traffic switched by BRC and Indiana Harbor Belt. Barr Yard is the largest of these, located in Riverdale along north of and adjacent to Indiana Harbor Belt's Blue Island Yard. This classification yard handles the majority of CSX's manifest traffic. On a typical day Barr originates ten trains and terminates five trains. Five outbound and seven inbound

CSX 917 leads a manifest train through Blue Island interlocking on the joint Indiana Harbor Belt/B&OCT trackage. In the background is CP Train 800 with two former Soo Line SD60s for power. This loaded coke train is headed for the Indiana Rail Road and will turn at Dolton to proceed south on Union Pacific's Villa Grove Subdivision to Indiana. *Matt Lastovich*

manifests daily serve Belt Railway's Clearing Yard. Indiana Harbor Belt's Gibson Yard terminates three automotive trains.

Bedford Park (located southwest of downtown parallel to BRC's Clearing Yard) is CSX's primary Chicago intermodal terminal, with a dozen outbound trains and fourteen inbound trains daily. Trains reaching Bedford Park use the Indiana Harbor Belt/B&OCT line via Blue Island. Most trains run via the Barr Subdivision heading east toward Gary, Indiana, except for a pair heading south from Dolton via UP's Villa Grove Subdivision.

CSX's 59th Street Yard (the former Pennsylvania Railroad yard located north of the 75th Street interlocking on the Blue Island Subdivision) sees six outbound and seven inbound trains daily. Also, a pair of trains run through to BNSF via the Ash Street connection north of Brighton Park. Two outbound and three inbound trains use the joint-with-UP Villa Grove Subdivision, and the balance operate east from Dolton on the Barr Subdivision.

This view from Baltimore & Ohio Chicago Terminal's South Branch bascule bridge shows the lay of the land to the west. At the center, B&OCT's bridge over Chicago Union Station and BNSF trackage, used by passenger trains to Grand Central Station until 1969, trails off into nothingness. The B&OCT track elevation west of BNSF 14th Street shops (still called the Zephyr Pit by veteran employees, and which service trains for Aurora and Manhattan), was demolished in 2004 to facilitate the University Village development along Halsted Street, visible in the distance beyond the elevated Dan Ryan Expressway. To the left the elevated St. Charles Air Line descends to a connection with UP (ex-C&NW and successor to the original St. Charles Air Line company) and BNSF at Union Avenue interlocking. Amtrak trains on the Illinois Central and BNSF and UP trains connecting with IC use this route. *Chris Guss*

CSX interchanges bulk and manifest trains with BNSF near the latter's Western Avenue Yard off the north end of the Blue Island Subdivision in Chicago. Bulk and manifest interchange with Union Pacific runs via IHB's main line between Blue Island and the east end of UP's former C&NW yard at Proviso. BRC's Rockwell Street Yard just east of Clearing Yard is the preferred Canadian National and Canadian Pacific interchange for bulk trains, including ethanol. Coal trains bound for the South Shore are interchanged at Miller (just east of Gary, Indiana).

CSX obtained control of CN's Elsdon Subdivision in 2013 as part of a deal that gave CN control of a portion of its Chicago–New Orleans main line (previously dispatched by CSX between Leewood and Aulon, Tennessee). CSX now dispatches approximately twenty-two miles of the Elsdon Subdivision in the Chicago area from Munster, Indiana, north to Elsdon. It plans to rebuild this line in 2014 to improve routing flexibility. As of early 2014, CSX operates six to eight trains a day across the Elsdon Sub, but when the upgrade is completed, CSX expects to run northbound traffic to Bedford Park on the Elsdon and outbound traffic southbound via the Indiana Harbor Belt at the west end of Bedford Park. New crossovers will be installed north of Blue Island between the Blue Island and Elsdon Subdivisions under this plan.

Norfolk Southern

Norfolk Southern operates two primary east-west routes into the Chicago area. The former Conrail Chicago Line is the busier of the two, but the Chicago District (former Nickel Plate Road) plays an important role.

The Chicago Line integrates portions of former New York Central's Lake Shore & Michigan Southern and PRR's Fort Wayne lines, stemming largely from changes made during the Penn Central and Conrail eras. North of Gary, Indiana, it runs in a northwesterly direction towards downtown Chicago on former New York Central right-of-way. Indiana Harbor Belt connects with the Chicago Line at CP502; it is one of busiest freight junctions on the route with dozens of NS, IHB, and Canadian Pacific trains using it daily. Further west, at CP505, the Chicago Line shifts southward to the former Pennsylvania Railroad alignment before reaching CP506 (site of Colehour Yard), and stays on the former PRR the remainder of the distance to 21st Street (near Union Station). At CP513 the line passes the former NYC Park Manor intermodal facility. Near the west end of that yard, at the site of the old Englewood Union Station, NS crosses Metra's Joliet Sub District (historically a level crossing, this was being grade-separated in 2013–2014). From Englewood the line turns north toward Chicago Union Station, passing 55th Street yard and CP518 where the CR&I Industrial Track swings west to serve Ashland Yard, Brighton Park, and Ash Street, terminating at Ogden Junction near the west end of Union Pacific's Global I Yard.

The Chicago District connects Fort Wayne, Indiana, and Chicago. Prior to the Conrail split in 1999, this was NS's primary Chicago main line, and although much of the traffic routed this way historically now operates via the Chicago Line to the north, the former Nickel Plate still hosts a sizeable volume of business, including traffic to and from the South, with Norfolk Southern shifting trains from one line to the other as necessary.

In addition to the east-west trunks, NS operates the Kankakee Line beginning at CP Highland and running south from the Chicago area, crossing the Canadian National's Matteson Subdivision (former EJ&E) at Hays. This route is primarily used by coal traffic and run-through trains to BNSF Railway at Streator, Illinois.

NS YARDS AND OPERATIONS

Although outside the Chicago terminal, NS's sprawling former Conrail (née New York Central) Elkhart terminal serves as a classification yard for Chicago traffic. Elkhart sees approximately thirteen daily carload trains in each direction carrying run-through traffic to and from Chicago-area connections. A few

A mid-1990s aerial view of Norfolk & Western's former Nickel Plate Road Calumet Yard. The roundhouse was among the last in the Chicago area. Today, this yard serves as a terminal for Norfolk Southern manifest and intermodal traffic. *Sean Graham-White*

Above: Norfolk Southern GP38-2 No. 5072 nears the end of another roundtrip with the bottle train on April 15, 2013. This train hauls molten steel from ArcelorMittal's Indiana Harbor blast furnaces to ArcelorMittal's Riverdale, Illinois plant near CSX's Barr Yard. The rear of the train is coming off the north end of Norfolk Southern's Kankakee Line after traversing IHB trackage from Dolton. The fifth car in the train is crossing CN's Lakefront Subdivision (ex-EJ&E), while the rear of the train is crossing NS's former New York Central Chicago Line within the CP 502 control point. *Chris Guss;* **Below:** Union Pacific 9448 leads a freight westbound at Arlington Heights on June 29, 2011. The three-track Harvard Subdivision has directional signaling on the outside tracks and bi-directional automatic block signaling on the center track that allows for movements in either direction on signal indication. UP installed C&NW-era ATS (automatic train stop) cab signal equipment on a handful of its General Electric C40-8Ws to lead trains in the Chicago area. As of 2014 these were the only DASH 8 locomotives still operating on Union Pacific. *Don Kalkman*

manifest trains use the former Nickel Plate Calumet Yard, while about four trains use the former NKP Chicago District.

The majority of NS's Chicago-area traffic involves intermodal containers moving through various terminals: 55th Street Yard, originating four eastbound trains and terminating five westbounds; Ashland Avenue Yard, handling four run-through trains each way for BNSF; Park Manor Yard, with five eastbounds and four westbounds; Landers Yard, handling four outbound and inbound trains; Calumet Yard, with two outbound and three inbound intermodal trains; and Colehour Yard, terminating a pair of trains.

Many NS trains run through to UP and BNSF. BNSF delivers several eastbound intermodal trains at Ashland Avenue. Westbound, two trains operate directly to BNSF's former Santa Fe Corwith Yard; a third runs further west on BNSF's Chillicothe Subdivision to deliver to BNSF's Willow Springs Yard, while a fourth goes to BNSF's former Burlington Northern Cicero Yard. Two intermodal trains operate directly to UP's Global I Yard.

In late 2013, Norfolk Southern discontinued operating RoadRailers into Chicago with the exception of a pair of run-through trains to Union Pacific that operate to Minneapolis, Minnesota. These run between UP's Proviso and Calumet Yards via Pullman Junction to Chicago Ridge, and then take the Indiana Harbor Belt to Proviso.

The most unusual NS operations are the daily molten steel shuttles running "hot bottle cars" from ArcelorMittal's blast furnaces in Northwest Indiana (the former Inland Steel mill near CP502 on Norfolk Southern's Chicago Line) across the Indiana Harbor Belt via Gibson to Dolton, and then via a surviving portion of the former Pennsylvania Railroad Panhandle Line to reach ArcelorMittal's Riverdale, Illinois, plant.

Union Pacific

Union Pacific's prominent Chicago presence is the function of key mergers with connecting lines in the last three decades combining its historic routes with Chicago & North Western, Missouri Pacific, and Southern Pacific. In 2013, UP's six routes into Chicago, plus a seventh via trackage rights on BNSF (see above), gave it more access than any other Class 1 freight line.

YARDS

The sixty-six-track Proviso hump is UP's primary Chicago area classification yard, making eighteen to twenty-four trains daily. UP also operates five Chicago intermodal yards. Global I, a former Chicago & North Western yard at the south end of UP's 2.3-mile Rockwell Subdivision from Kedzie to Canal Street (just east of Ogden Junction) handles four to six trains daily. Global II, a sprawling facility adjacent to Proviso, sees six to eight through trains daily and shuttles from other Chicago intermodal facilities. Global III, located near Rochelle, Illinois, at milepost 75.9 on the Geneva Subdivision, conducts block swapping and loads agricultural products for export. Global IV, a modern 785-acre intermodal ramp near Joliet (the yard's northern end is in Joliet with the balance of the facility in the adjacent town of Elwood), opened in 2013 so UP could phase out the old Missouri Pacific Canal Street intermodal yard. The Yard Center intermodal facility (south of Dolton interlocking), a former Missouri Pacific yard on the former Chicago & Eastern Illinois route

A Union Pacific manifest glides eastbound over former Chicago & North Western trackage at West Chicago on Union Pacific's Geneva Subdivision. The diamonds in the foreground are the former EJ&E, now Canadian National's Leithton Subdivision. *Matt Lastovich*

(UP's Villa Grove Subdivision) handles six to eight daily intermodal trains between Texas and Mexico. In December 2013 UP announced it would serve an industrial park near Coal City, Illinois, on the former Alton.

PRINCIPAL CHICAGO ROUTES

Union Pacific's busiest route is the Geneva Subdivision, the former C&NW east-west main line line to Omaha/Council Bluffs. It is a primary corridor for Powder River coal, transcontinental carload freight, and intermodal traffic. The Geneva Sub is protected by cab signals, so only locomotives fitted with UP's cab-signal equipment are allowed to lead trains. UP's West Chicago yard features a small automotive ramp along with a switching yard where several locals are based. The 47.3-mile Belvidere Subdivision, another former C&NW line, diverges at West Chicago running west via Union, Illinois, (location of the Illinois Railway Museum) toward its namesake Illinois town to serve a Chrysler assembly plant.

The Harvard Subdivision runs from Clinton Street interlocking in downtown Chicago northwesterly, via its namesake, towards Janesville, Wisconsin. This line features a mixture of ABS and CTC signal territory, with three main tracks from CY to Barrington (crossing Canadian National's Leithton Subdivision, the former EJ&E). West of Barrington, it has two main tracks to Harvard. At Crystal Lake Junction, the eleven-mile McHenry Subdivision, used by Metra commuter trains to McHenry, diverges north toward Ringwood. A local freight based at South Janesville Yard works industries in this area. In commuter territory, the Harvard route is equipped with an Automatic Train Stop (ATS) signal system dating from C&NW days; only a handful of UP locomotives are equipped to lead freight trains in ATS territory.

Two former C&NW lines connect Chicago and Milwaukee. The first is UP's Milwaukee Subdivision, extending ninety-three miles from Grand Avenue near north end of Yard 9 in Proviso Yard to Milwaukee's Butler Yard. (Traditionally, as discussed in Chapter 1, this was known as the New Line.) In addition to carload freights, this route handles coal for power plants in northern Illinois and southern Wisconsin, and occasionally unit sand and

The Central Illinois Railroad leased from BNSF trackage in and around the Lumber District, including the lone remnant of the narrow gauge Chicago, Millington & Western. The operation lasted only ten years before BNSF resumed operation of the lines in 2010. Central Illinois SW1200 1206 switches out a customer on April 8, 2010, exactly four months before operations would revert back to BNSF. *John Ryan*

At 26th Street, Belt Railway of Chicago's north-south line toward Cragin crosses over BNSF's Chicago Sub just east of Cicero Yard. To the left of BRC is Manufacturers Junction Railway's elevated line. In this view from the mid-1990s, one of MJ's switchers can be spotted between green plate girder spans on its viaduct. *Sean Graham-White*

grain trains. Parallel to the Milwaukee Sub is UP's Kenosha Subdivision, the original former C&NW line, running eighty miles from Chicago (Ogilvie Transportation Center) to St. Francis on the south side of Milwaukee. Most of the line is equipped with Automatic Train Stop with Automatic Cab Signal (ACS) overlaid from Lake Bluff north. ACS allows UP coal and freight trains to operate without adding an ATS-equipped locomotive in Chicago before entering the Kenosha Subdivision at Lake Bluff, off the Lake Subdivision. Locals are based in Waukegan at an eleven-track yard. Connecting the Milwaukee and Kenosha Subs north of Chicago is the 1.9-mile Lake Subdivision running from control point KO (formerly Skokie Junction) on the Milwaukee Subdivision to Lake Bluff. This route primarily provides access to the Kenosha Subdivision north of

Lake Bluff for coal trains to the Midwest Generation plant at Waukegan, Illinois, and the WE Energies plant at Oak Creek, Wisconsin.

The former C&EI main line is operated as UP's Villa Grove Subdivision, running from 81st Street to Jay Tower. This line handles Chicago–Texas–Mexico traffic. As discussed above, CSX operates over this line for sixty-six miles between Dolton and Woodland Junction, a legacy of Louisville & Nashville's expansion into Chicago.

Terminal Railroads and Short Lines
BELT RAILWAY OF CHICAGO
Belt Railway of Chicago is owned by the six Class 1 railroads serving Chicago, which use this key property to classify cars and route traffic through the city. BRC operates a twenty-eight-mile main line from Norfolk Southern's Chicago Line at CP509

An eastbound Chicago Rail Link train passes over the Dan Ryan Expressway and CTA's Red Line as it heads towards Pullman Junction on February 17, 2012. This OmniTRAX-owned railroad has an eclectic roster of locomotives, with a GP50, GP15-1, and GP35 working here. CRL operates the former Rock Island trackage east from Gresham Interlocking to connections with eastern carriers at 95th Street. *Marshall W. Beecher*

(southeast of downtown) to Cragin on the northwest side of the city, where it connects to Canadian Pacific's (former Milwaukee Road) Elgin Subdivision. Critical to BRC's operations, Clearing Yard is 5.5 miles long, covers 786 acres, and features a massive double hump. In addition, BRC operates Clearing-based locals, plus a switcher based in South Chicago at 100th Street Yard for local industries and the nearby KCBX coal-to-water terminal.

CHICAGO, FT. WAYNE & EASTERN

Chicago, Ft. Wayne & Eastern operates a single train into Chicago using a portion of the former PRR Fort Wayne route. At Tolleston, CF&E trains run three miles via CSXs Porter Subdivision reaching IHB at Ivanhoe, where trains continue to IHB's Blue Island yard for interchange.

CHICAGO RAIL LINK

Chicago Rail Link (CRL) operates seventy-two miles from UP's Global I intermodal yard to Union Avenue, east to 16th Street Tower, then south on Metra's former Rock Island Joliet Sub District from 16th Street to suburban Mokena. Off this core route, it serves a segment of the Joliet Sub running from Root Street west to Ashland Avenue on Norfolk Southern. Immediately east of Gresham, CRL extends east to South Chicago, south from Pullman Junction to Kensington, and from just west of Rock Island Junction to South Deering, where the Irondale Yard and shops are located. Regular operations include a local running most days from Irondale to Iowa Interstate's Burr Oak yard in Blue Island. CRL also services customers along Metra's Joliet Sub District to Mokena. Occasionally, Iowa Interstate interchanges ethanol trains with CRL to forward to Norfolk Southern.

CHICAGO TERMINAL RAILROAD

Chicago Terminal Railroad, owned by Iowa Pacific Holdings, operates three separate groups of industrial trackage on Chicago's north and west side: former Canadian Pacific (Milwaukee Road) trackage in the Goose Island area immediately north of downtown Chicago; the Centrex Industrial Park in Elk Grove Village adjacent to Union Pacific's Milwaukee Subdivision near Bryn Mawr; and Bensenville's Industrial Park (northwest of Canadian Pacific's Bensenville Yard).

GARY RAILWAY

When Canadian National acquired the Elgin Joliet & Eastern Railroad in 2009, EJ&E's sixty-three miles of trackage within the Gary Works were not included in the sale. U.S. Steel retained control of this trackage, operating it as the Gary Railway.

INDIANA HARBOR BELT

Indiana Harbor Belt remains one of the city's primary belt lines, providing connections and terminal facilities for Class 1 railroads (see Chapter 1) in addition to serving local

Above: A Chicago Terminal SW9 spots a load for Big Bay Lumber in the middle of Cherry Street on Goose Island. This former Milwaukee Road trackage was once part of an extensive network serving dozens of customers on the Near North Side of Chicago. Today, most industries have left the area, and the few remaining rail patrons are switched on an as-needed basis by trains originating at Union Pacific's North Yard. *Matt Lastovich;* **Below:** A northbound Indiana Harbor Belt train passes by Calumet Tower and the crossing of B&OCT's Barr Subdivision. Calumet Tower closed as result of the CREATE program, transferring control of this interlocking to IHB's East Dispatcher. A month after closure in March 2013, the tower was demolished. *Matt Lastovich*

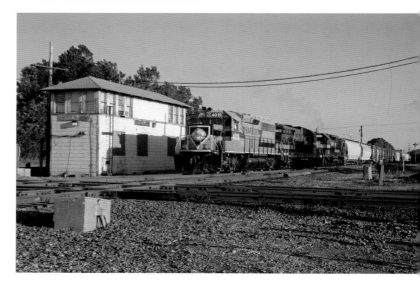

On May 5, 2011, BNSF SD70MAC No. 9876 passes by the closed Hohman Avenue Tower on the IHB main line. The train is eastbound toward Gibson Yard with a long cut of autoracks for classification. The train will cross the former Nickel Plate main line seen at the upper right corner of the photo, which is Norfolk Southern's Chicago District today. The through-truss bridge in the trees above the train once hosted Monon, Chesapeake & Ohio, and Erie/Erie Lackawanna trains across diamonds that were located immediately in front of the locomotive. *Chris Guss*

customers. It operates four primary yards: Norpaul Yard, at the far north end of the railroad; Blue Island Yard, between Blue Island and Dolton, the primary classification yard for car load traffic, with a hump sorting cars into a forty-four-track bowl (several railroads use IHB's Blue Island as a Chicago area terminal); Gibson Yard at Hammond Indiana; and Michigan Avenue Yard, which primarily supports the local steel mills. Gibson Yard is also the railroad's primary locomotive shop, featuring one of the few surviving roundhouses in the Chicago area.

INDIANA RAIL ROAD

In 2006 Indiana Rail Road acquired the remaining trackage of the Milwaukee Road's old Southeastern lines from Canadian Pacific. Included in the deal were haulage rights over CSX between Chicago and Terre Haute, Indiana. INRD trains operate over the former C&EI through Jay Tower and Dolton to 80th Street and then north to the CP interchange at Cragin via Belt Railway of Chicago. As of 2014, INRD's Chicago area appearances remained sporadic, consisting primarily of unit coke trains from Roseport, Minnesota (near

Minneapolis), to Indiana that are interchanged with CP at Galewood Yard on the Elgin Subdivision. CSX hauls INRD carload traffic in its own trains.

IOWA INTERSTATE

Iowa Interstate Railroad (IAIS) operates freight service on the former Rock Island east-west main line between Chicago and Council Bluffs, Iowa. In the Chicago area, it has trackage rights on the former Rock route, now operated by Metra between Blue Island and Joliet, then west to Bureau over CSXs New Rock Subdivision. Beyond Bureau, the former Rock is now controlled by IAIS. Typically, IAIS has one scheduled daily road freight serving the Chicago area, terminating at Burr Oak Yard in Blue Island. Other services, such as occasional ethanol trains, are delivered to Chicago Rail Link or CSX for forwarding to the East Coast. A Burr Oak–based local handles customers between Blue Island and Joliet along with interchange traffic to IHB's Blue Island Yard.

Indiana Rail Road provides some of Chicago's most elusive trains. Its access to Chicago is a carryover from Milwaukee Road's Indiana extension, dating from 1921, when predecessor St. Paul leased the Chicago, Terre Haute & Southeastern Railway to reach southern Indiana coal mines. Most of Milwaukee's Indiana route has been abandoned, and CSX now operates INRD's trains to Chicago to connect with Milwaukee successor Canadian Pacific. In this view, INRD SD90/43MACs lead CP Train 800 on the C&M Subdivision at Gurnee, Illinois. *Chris Guss*

Crossing the Calumet Sag Channel, an inbound Iowa Interstate train has just doubled out of Evans Yard and eases its way towards the west end of Burr Oak Yard in Blue Island on April 20, 2012. The former Rock Island Yard is Iowa Interstate's operating base in the Chicago area. *Chris Guss*

SOUTH CHICAGO AND INDIANA HARBOR RAILWAY

In 2002, International Steel Group acquired the former Chicago Short Line Railway (see Chapter 1) and renamed it South Chicago and Indiana Harbor Railway. This carrier, primarily handling coke shipments for ArcelorMittal, operates five miles of Illinois-based trackage (near the Illinois-Indiana state line) extending west from a junction with Norfolk Southern's Chicago Line at CP509 to Pullman Junction, and industrial trackage north of NS's line and on the east side of the Calumet River, plus twenty-three miles of trackage on NS and CSX lines in the heavily industrialized area around Indiana Harbor. Its trains still carry

cabooses to assist with reverse operations necessary for switching.

WISCONSIN & SOUTHERN

The Wisconsin and Southern Railroad operates a daily road freight from its Janesville, Wisconsin, hub over the former Milwaukee Road route to Belt Railway's Clearing Yard. Today, this consists of trackage rights on Metra from Fox Lake, Illinois, to Rondout (junction with Canadian Pacific's C&M Subdivision), then trackage rights on CP's lines toward Chicago. WSOR trains run to Tower A-5 (Pacific Junction), then follow CP's east-west Elgin Subdivision 1.3 miles to Cragin, where they enter BRC's line to Clearing. The lack of a direct connection at Cragin requires a reverse move.

Left: When not in use, South Chicago and Indiana Harbor Railway's immaculate fleet of locomotives resides in the shops near CP509 on Norfolk Southern's Chicago Line. Still lettered for their predecessor, Chicago Short Line, the new company hasn't changed the look of the railroad since its takeover in 2002. Locomotive 28 is an EMD model SW1001s that features a low-cab profile for use in tight industrial areas. *Ryan Schoenfeldt;* **Below:** Wisconsin & Southern is one of several Midwestern railroads spawned by Milwaukee Road's retrenchment in the 1980s. Although most of its operations are centered in southern Wisconsin, it runs nightly road freights between its Janesville, Wisconsin, hub and BRC's Clearing Yard. On August 22, 2012, eastbound train T-002 shoves by the former Milwaukee Road A5 Tower at Pacific Junction. When this tower was commissioned on August 15, 1942, it controlled approximately two hundred moves a day through the plant. Since that time, a few tracks have been removed and the diamond crossing lifted. The former Chicago & Pacific east of A5 is being converted into an elevated hiking trail. *Marshall W. Beecher*

Bibliography

Books

_____. *1846–1896 Fiftieth Anniversary of the Incorporation of the Pennsylvania Railroad Company*. Philadelphia: Pennsylvania Railroad Company, 1896.

_____. *Organization and Traffic of the Illinois Central System*. Chicago: Illinois Central Railroad Company, 1938.

_____. *Interurban to Milwaukee: Bulletin 103*. Chicago: Central Electric Railfans' Association, 1962.

_____. *All Stations: A Journey Through 150 Years of Railway History*. Paris, [country or state]: 1978.

_____. *Encyclopedia of American Business History and Biography: Railroads in the Nineteenth Century*. New York: Bruccoli Clark Layman and Facts on File, 1988.

Abbey, Wallace W. *The Little Jewel*. Pueblo, CO: Pinon Productions, 1984.

Angle, Paul M. (ed.) *The Great Chicago Fire: The Human Account*. Chicago: The Chicago Historical Society, 1946.

Arnold, Bion Joseph. *Report on the Rearrangement and Development of the Steam Railroad Terminals in the City of Chicago*. Chicago: Citizens' Terminal Plan Committee, 1913.

Baedeker, Karl. *Baedeker's The United States: Handbook for Travelers*. Leipzig: Karl Baedeker Publishing, 1909.

Bancroft, Hubert Howe. *The Book of the Fair: An Historical and Descriptive Presentation of the World's Science, Art, and Industry, as Viewed Through the Columbian Exposition at Chicago in 1893 (reprint)*. Chicago: Bounty Books, 1974.

Blaszak, Michael W. *Baltimore & Ohio Chicago Terminal: An Historical Sketch*. Unpublished Monograph, 1993.

Borzo, Greg. *The Chicago "L."* Mount Pleasant, SC: Arcadia Publishing, 2007.

Bryant, Keith L. *History of the Atchison, Topeka & Santa Fe Railway*. New York: Macmillan, 1974.

Bryant Jr., Keith L. *Railroads in the Age of Regulation, 1900–1980*. New York: Bruccoli Clark Layman and Facts on File, 1988.

Buell, L. A. *The Santa Fe in Illinois*. Unpublished Monograph, 1993.

Burch, Edward P. *Electric Traction for Railway Trains*. New York: McGraw-Hill, 1911.

Burgess, George H., and Miles C. Kennedy. *Centennial History of the Pennsylvania Railroad*. Philadelphia: Pennsylvania Railroad Company, 1949.

Bush, Donald J. *The Streamlined Decade*. New York, George Braziller, 1975.

Cary, John W. *The Organization and History of The Chicago, Milwaukee & St. Paul Railway Company*. New York: Arno Press, 1981.

Casey, Robert J., and Douglas, W. A. S. *Pioneer Railroad: The Story of the Chicago and North Western System*. New York: McGraw-Hill, 1948.

Chicago & North Western Railway. *Yesterday and Today: A History of the Chicago and North Western Railway System, 3rd Edition (reprint)*. Chicago: Chicago Chapter, Railway & Locomotive Historical Society, 1981.

Chicago, Milwaukee, St. Paul & Pacific Railroad Company. *The Milwaukee Road: A Brief History*. Milwaukee, WI: Milwaukee Road Public Relations Department, 1968.

Churella, Albert, J. *From Steam to Diesel*. Princeton, NJ: Princeton University Press, 1998.

City of Chicago Committee on Railway Terminals. *The Railway Passenger Terminal Problem at Chicago.* Chicago: City of Chicago Committee on Railway Terminals, 1933.

Committee of Investigation on Smoke Abatement and Electrification of Railway Terminals. *Smoke Abatement and Electrification of Railway Terminals in Chicago.* Chicago: Rand McNally, 1915.

Corliss, Carlton J. *Main Line of Mid-America: The Story of the Illinois Central.* [city]: Creative Age Press, 1950.

Currie, A. W. *The Grand Trunk Railway of Canada.* Toronto: University of Toronto Press, 1957.

Daughen, Joseph R., and Peter Binzen. *The Wreck of the Penn Central.* Boston: Little, Brown, 1971.

DeBoer, David J. *Piggyback and Containers.* San Marino, CA: Golden West Books, 1992.

Del Grosso, Robert C. *Burlington Northern 1980–1991 Annual.* Denver: Hyrail Publications, 1991.

Doherty, Timothy Scott, and Brian Solomon. *Conrail.* St. Paul, MN: MBI Publishing, 2004.

Dolzall, Gary W., and Stephen F. Dolzall. *Monon: The Hoosier Line.* Glendale, CA: Interurban Press, 1987.

Dorsey, Edward Bates. *English and American Railroads Compared.* New York: John Wiley & Sons, 1887.

Droege, John A. *Freight Terminals and Trains.* New York: McGraw-Hill, 1912.

———. *Passenger Terminals and Trains.* New York: McGraw-Hill, 1916.

Drury, George H. *The Historical Guide to North American Railroads.* Waukesha, WI: Kalmbach Books, 1985.

———. *The Train Watcher's Guide to North American Railroads.* Waukesha, WI: Kalmbach Books, 1992.

———. *Guide to North American Steam Locomotives.* Waukesha, WI: Kalmbach Books, 1993.

Dunbar, Willis F. *Michigan: A History of the Wolverine State.* Wm. B. Eerdmans Publishing Co., 1965.

Dubin, Arthur D. *Some Classic Trains.* Milwaukee, WI: Kalmbach Publishing, 1964.

———. *More Classic Trains.* Milwaukee, WI: Kalmbach Publishing, 1974.

Farrington Jr., S. Kip. *Railroading from the Head End.* New York: Doubleday, Doran & Co., 1943.

———. *Railroading from the Rear End.* New York: Coward McKann, 1946.

———. *Railroads of Today.* New York: Coward McKann, 1949.

———. *Railroading the Modern Way.* New York: Coward McKann, 1951.

———. *Railroads of the Hour.* New York: Coward McKann, 1958.

Glendinning, Gene V. *The Chicago & Alton Railroad: The Only Way.* DeKalb, IL: Northern Illinois University Press, 2002.

Grant, H. Roger. *The Corn Belt Route: A History of the Chicago Great Western Railroad Company.* DeKalb, IL: Northern Illinois University Press, 1984.

———. *Erie Lackawanna: Death of an American Railroad, 1938–1992.* Stanford, CA: Stanford University Press, 1994.

———. *The North Western: A History of the Chicago & North Western Railway System.* DeKalb, IL: Northern Illinois University Press, 1996.

Grant, H. Roger. *Follow the Flag: A History of the Wabash Railroad Company.* [city]: Northern Illinois Press, 2004.

Gruber, John. *Focus on Rails*. North Freedom, WI: Mid-Continent Railway Historical Society, 1989.

_____. *Railroad History in a Nutshell*. Madison, WI: Center for Railroad Photography and Art, 2009.

_____. *Railroad Preservation in a Nutshell*. Madison, WI: Center for Railroad Photography and Art, 2011.

Gruber, John, and Brian Solomon. *The Milwaukee Road's Hiawathas*. St. Paul, MN: MBI, 2006.

Hampton, Taylor. *The Nickel Plate Road*. Cleveland, OH: World Publishing, 1947.

Harlow, Alvin F. *The Road of the Century*. New York: Creative Age Press, 1947.

Hayes, William Edward. *Iron Road to Empire: The History of the Rock Island Lines*. Wolfe Book Company, 1953.

Hilton, George W. *American Narrow Gauge Railroads*. Stanford, CA: Stanford University Press, 1990.

_____. *The Cable Car in America*. San Diego, CA: Howell-North Books, 1982.

_____. *The Great Lakes Car Ferries*. Howell-North Books, 1962.

_____. *Monon Route*. Howell-North Books, n.d.

_____. *The Cable Car in America (rev. ed.)*, Palo Alto, CA: Stanford University Press, 1997.

Hilton, George W., and John F Due. *The Electric Interurban Railways in America*. Palo Alto, CA: Stanford University Press, 1960 (paperback edition 2000).

Hofsommer, Don L. *Grand Trunk Corporation: Canadian National Railways in the United States,   1971–1992*. East Lansing, MI: Michigan State University Press, 1995.

Holbrook, Stewart H. *The Story of American Railroads*. New York: Crown, 1947.

Holland, Rupert Sargent. *Historic Railroads*. Philadelphia: Macrae Smith Company, 1927.

Howard, Robert P. *Illinois: A History of the Prairie State*. Wm. B. Eerdmans Publishing Co., 1972.

Hoyt, Edwin P. *The Vanderbilts and Their Fortunes*. New York: Doubleday & Company, 1962.

Hungerford, Edward. *Daniel Willard Rides the Line*. New York: G. P. Putnam's Sons, 1938.

_____. *Men of Erie*. New York: Random House, 1946.

Ivey, Paul Wesley. *The Pere Marquette Railroad Company*. Grand Rapids, MI: The Black Letter Press, 1970.

Johnson, Emory, R. *American Railway Transportation*. New York: D. Appleton and Company, 1910.

Johnson, F. H. *The Milwaukee Road 1847–1944*. Milwaukee, WI: Milwaukee Road Public Relations Department, 1944.

Johnson, James D. *A Century of Chicago Streetcars 1858–1958*. Wheaton, IL: The Traction Orange Company, 1964.

Klein, Maury. *Union Pacific, Vols. I &II*. New York: Doubleday, 1989.

_____. *Union Pacific: The Reconfiguration: America's Greatest Railroad from 1969 to the Present*. New York: Oxford University Press, 2011.

Knoll, Charles M. *Go Pullman*. Rochester, NY: Rochester Chapter, National Railway Historical Society, 1995.

Krambles, George (ed.). *The Great Third Rail*. Chicago: Central Electric Railfans' Association, 1961.

Lamb, W. Kaye. *History of the Canadian Pacific Railway*. New York: Macmillan, 1977.

Leider, David J. *The Wisconsin Central in Illinois*. Prospect Heights, IL: David J. Leider, 2010.

Lemly, James H. *The Gulf, Mobile & Ohio*. Homewood, IL: Richard D. Irwin, 1953.

Lind, Alan R. *Chicago Surface Lines: An Illustrated History, 3rd Edition*. Park Forest, IL: Transport History Press, 1979.

_____. *Limiteds Along the Lakefront: The Illinois Central in Chicago*. Park Forest, IL: Transport History Press, 1986.

_____. *From the Lakes to the Gulf: The Illinois Central Story*. Park Forest, IL: Transport History Press, 1993.

Marre, Louis A., and Jerry A. Pinkepank. *The Contemporary Diesel Spotter's Guide*. Milwaukee: Kalmbach Publications, 1985.

_____. *Diesel Locomotives: The First 50 Years.* Waukesha, WI: Kalmbach Publications, 1995.

Marshall, James. *Santa Fe: The Railroad That Built an Empire.* New York: Random House, 1945.

Mayer, Harold Melvin. *The Railway Pattern of Metropolitan Chicago.* Chicago: University of Chicago Press, 1943.

Mayer, Harold M., and Richard C. Wade. *Chicago: Growth of a Metropolis.* Chicago: University of Chicago Press, 1969.

McDonald, Charles W. *Diesel Locomotive Rosters.* Milwaukee, WI: Kalmbach, 1982.

McLellan, Dave, and Bill Warrick. *The Lake Shore & Michigan Southern Railway.* Polo, IL: Transportation Trails, 1989.

Meeks, Carroll L. V. *The Railroad Station.* New Haven, CT: Yale University Press, 1956.

Middleton, William D. *When the Steam Railroads Electrified.* Milwaukee, WI: Kalmbach, 1974.

_____. *North Shore: America's Fastest Interurban.* San Marino, CA: Golden West Books, 1964.

_____. *Time of the Trolley.* Milwaukee, WI: Kalmbach Publishing,1967.

_____. *South Shore: The Last Interurban.* San Marino, CA: Golden West Books, 1970.

_____. *Landmarks on the Iron Road.* Bloomington, IN: Indiana University Press, 1999.

_____. *Metropolitan Railways: Rapid Transit in America.* Bloomington, IN: Indiana University Press, 2003.

Middleton, William D., with George M. Smerk and Roberta L. Diehl. *Encyclopedia of North American Railroads.* Bloomington, IN: Indiana University Press, 2007.

Mott, Edward Harold. *Between the Ocean and the Lakes: The Story of Erie.* New York: John S. Collins, 1900.

New York Central System. *Corporate History of the Cleveland, Cincinnati, Chicago & St. Louis Railway Company (reprint).* Gates Mills, OH: New York Central Historical Society, n.d.

Overton, Richard C. *Burlington West.* Cambridge, MA: Harvard University Press, 1941.

_____. *Burlington Route.* New York: Alfred A. Knopf, 1965.

Pearson, J. P. *Railways and Scenery: Series 1, Volumes I–IV.* London: Cassell and Company, 1932.

Pere Marquette Railway Company. *The Pere Marquette in 1945 (reprint).* Clifton Forge, VA: Chesapeake & Ohio Historical Society, 1990.

Potter, Janet Greenstein. *Great American Railroad Stations.* New York: John Wiley & Sons, 1996.

Protheroe, Ernest. *The Railways of the World.* London: George Routledge & Sons, 1920.

Quiett, Glenn Chesney. *They Built the West.* New York: D. Appleton-Century, 1934.

Rehor, John A. *The Nickel Plate Story, 4th printing.* Milwaukee, WI: Kalmbach Publishing, 1965.

Saunders Jr., Richard. *The Railroad Mergers and the Coming of Conrail.* Westport, CT: Greenwood-Heineman Publishing, 1978.

_____. *Merging Lines: American Railroads 1900–1970.* DeKalb, IL: Northern Illinois University Press, 2001.

_____. *Main Lines: American Railroads 1970–2002.* DeKalb, IL: Northern Illinois University Press, 2003.

Schafer, Mike, and Brian Solomon. *Pennsylvania Railroad.* Minneapolis, MN: Voyageur Press, 2009.

Simons, Richard S., and Francis H. Parker. *Railroads of Indiana.* Bloomington, IN: Indiana University Press, 1997.

Solomon, Brian. *The American Steam Locomotive.* Osceola, WI: MBI, 1998.

_____. *The American Diesel Locomotive.* Osceola, WI: MBI, 2000.

_____. *Railway Masterpieces: Celebrating the World's Greatest Trains, Stations and Feats of Engineering.* Iola, WI: Krause Publishing, 2002.

_____. *Railroad Signaling.* St. Paul, MN: MBI, 2003.

_____. *Amtrak.* St. Paul, MN: MBI, 2004.

_____. *Burlington Northern Santa Fe Railway.* St. Paul, MN: MBI, 2005.

_____. *CSX*. St. Paul, MN: MBI, 2005.

North American Railroad: The Illustrated Encyclopedia. Minneapolis, MN: Voyageur Press, 2012.

Solomon, Brian, and Mike Schafer. *New York Central Railroad*. Osceola, WI: MBI, 1999.

Stover, John F. *The Life and Decline of the American Railroad*. New York: Oxford University Press, 1970.

_____. *History of the Illinois Central Railroad*. New York: Macmillan Publishing, 1975.

_____. *History of the Baltimore & Ohio Railroad*. West Lafayette, IN: Purdue University Press, 1987.

_____. *The Routledge Historical Atlas of the American Railroads*. New York: Routledge, 1999.

Swengel, Frank M. *The American Steam Locomotive: Volume 1, Evolution*. Davenport, IA: Midwest Rail Publications, 1967.

Talbot, F. A. *Railway Wonders of the World, Volumes 1 & 2*. London: Cassell & Company, 1914.

Turner, Charles W., Thomas W. Dixon Jr., and Eugene L. Huddleston. *Chessie's Road*. Clifton Forge, VA: Chesapeake & Ohio Historical Society, 1986.

Vance Jr., James E. *The North American Railroad*. Baltimore: Johns Hopkins University Press, 1995.

Wade, Louise Carroll. *Chicago's Pride: The Stockyards, Packingtown and Environs in the Nineteenth Century*. Champaign, IL: University of Illinois Press, 1987.

Walker, Mike. *Steam Powered Video's Comprehensive Railroad Atlas of North America: Great Lakes West, U.S.A.* Feaversham, Kent, UK: Steam Powered Publishing, 1996.

Waters, L. L. *Steel Trails to Santa Fe*. Lawrence, KS: University of Kansas Press, 1950.

Westing, Frederic, and Alvin F. Staufer. *Erie Power*. Medina, OH: A. F. Staufer, 1970.

White Jr., John H. *A History of the American Locomotive: Its Development: 1830–1880*. Baltimore: Johns Hopkins University Press, 1968.

_____. *The American Railroad Passenger Car, Volumes I & II*. Baltimore: Johns Hopkins University Press, 1978.

Winchester, Clarence. *Railway Wonders of the World, Volumes 1 & 2*. London: The Waverley Book Company, 1935.

Periodicals

American Railroad Journal and Mechnics' Magazine. Published in the 1830s and 1840s.

Baldwin Locomotives. Philadelphia, PA. No longer published.

CTC Board. Ferndale, WA.

Illinois Historical Society Journal. 1954.

Jane's World Railways. London.

Moody's Analyses of Investments, Part I: Steam Railroads. New York.

Moody's Transportation Manual. Various editions.

Official Guide to the Railways: 1868–1969. New York.

Pacific RailNews. Waukesha, WI. No longer published.

Poor's Manual of Railroads. Various editions.

Progressive Railroading. Milwaukee, WI.

Railroad History, formerly *Railway and Locomotive Historical Society Bulletin*. Boston, MA.

Railway and Locomotive Engineering. New York. No longer published.

Railway Age. Chicago and New York.

Railway Gazette: 1870–1908. New York. No longer published.

Railway Signaling and Communications, formerly *The Railway Signal Engineer,* née *Railway Signaling.* Chicago and New York.

The Milwaukee Railroader.

The Railway Gazette. London.

The Soo.

Trains. Waukesha, WI.

Vintage Rails. Waukesha, WI. No longer published.

Washington Post. Washington D.C.

Brochures, Manuals, Timetables, Rulebooks, and Reports

American Association of Railroads. *Intermodal Committee Loading Capabilities Guide.* 2005.

American Association of State Highway and Transportation Officials. *Freight-Rail Bottom Line Report.* 2003.

Amtrak public timetables 1971–2011.

Burlington Northern Santa Fe Corporation. *Annual Reports 1996–2004.*

Burlington Northern Santa Fe Railway. *System Map.* 2003.

Chicago, Milwaukee, St. Paul & Pacific public timetables 1943–1966.

Chicago Operating Rules Association. *Operating Guide.* 1994.

Erie Railroad. *Erie Railroad: Its Beginnings and Today.* 1951.

Interstate Commerce Commission. *Fourth Annual Report on the Statistics of Railways of the United States for the Year ended June 30, 1891.* Washington, D.C. 1892.

General Code of Operating Rules, Fourth Edition. 2000.

NORAC Operating Rules, 7th Edition. 2000.

Pennsylvania Railroad public timetables 1942–1968.

Santa Fe public timetables 1943–1969.

Internet Sources

metrarail.com

www.aar.org

www.bnsf.com

www.cn.ca

www.cpr.ca

www.csx.com

www.ctainc.com

www.fra.dot.gov

www.ihbrr.com

www.nscorp.com

www.railamerica.com

www.uprr.com

www.wsorrailro

www.wsorrailroad.com

Index